Cuba and the Missile Crisis

Cuba and the Missile Crisis

Carlos Lechuga

Translated by Mary Todd

OCEAN PRESS
Melbourne • New York

An earlier version of this book was published in 1995 under the title *In the Eye of the Storm — Castro, Khrushchev, Kennedy and the Missile Crisis*

Cover design by David Spratt

ISBN 1-876175-34-6

Printed in Australia

First printed 2001

Published by Ocean Press
Australia: GPO Box 3279, Melbourne, Victoria 3001, Australia
  • Fax: (61-3) 9329 5040 • E-mail: info@oceanbooks.com.au
USA: PO Box 1186, Old Chelsea Station, New York, NY 10113-1186, USA

Library of Congress Catalog Card No: 2001092675

OCEAN PRESS DISTRIBUTORS
United States & Canada: LPC Group,
   1436 West Randolph St, Chicago, IL 60607, USA
Britain and Europe: Global Book Marketing,
   38 King Street, London, WC2E 8JT, UK
Australia and New Zealand: Astam Books,
   57-61 John Street, Leichhardt, NSW 2040, Australia
Cuba and Latin America: Ocean Press,
   Calle 21 #406, Vedado, Havana, Cuba
Southern Africa: Phambili Agencies,
   PO Box 28680, Kensington 2101, Johannesburg, South Africa

www.oceanbooks.com.au

Contents

For my grandchildren

Carlos Lechuga

Carlos Lechuga Hevia was Cuba's ambassador to the United Nations at the time of the Missile Crisis and took an active part in some of the negotiations in that world forum.

After the crisis, he participated in the contacts Kennedy made with Fidel Castro — which many analysts consider were aimed at opening up channels for détente in U.S. relations with Cuba and which may have been one of the reasons for Kennedy's assassination.

Lechuga has carried out many diplomatic missions and has represented Cuba in numerous international conferences and activities.

He was Cuba's last ambassador to the Organization of American States and also served as ambassador to Chile, Mexico and Portugal.

Lechuga represented Cuba in several UN agencies in Geneva in 1971-78 and 1984-89. He has served as Vice-Chairman of the Human Rights Commission, Deputy Chairman of the First Commission of the General Assembly, President of the Disarmament Conference, elected President of the Negotiating Group on Radiological Weapons, member of the Consultative Board of Disarmament Studies (twice, under UN Secretaries-General Kurt Waldheim and Javier Pérez de Cuéllar), and member of the Group of Governmental Experts on Constitutional Disarmament Arrangements.

In 1994, he was reelected a member of the Committee of the Convention on the Elimination of Racial Discrimination and was elected Vice-Chairman of the Committee.

He was Coordinator of two UNCTADs of the Group of 77, in Manila and Geneva.

He was President of the National Council of Culture and, as such, a member of the Cuban Council of Ministers.

Journalist, diplomat and writer, his work has been published in Cuba, other Latin American countries and the United States. His book *Itinerario de una farsa* [Itinerary of a farce] won the 1992 critics award in Cuba.

1

The beginnings

N o one has determined the exact moment, the circumstances or even the place where it occurred to the Premier of the Soviet Union to propose to the government of Cuba that nuclear missiles be installed in its territory. Although this is not of any great historical importance, it does illustrate the fuzziness that characterizes the dramatic happenings of October 1962, which brought the world to the brink of an atomic war and the most serious crisis which humanity has faced since World War II.

The Cold War was at its height, international conflicts had broken out on all continents and the ideological struggle between the two largest powers was increasingly represented by inflammatory rhetoric.

That was the political climate in April 1962, when Nikita Khrushchev and Deputy Premier Anastas Mikoyan were walking in the garden behind Khrushchev's residence in the Lenin Hills just outside Moscow, an area reserved for the members of the Presidium. Khrushchev told Mikoyan he was thinking of proposing to the government of Cuba that medium- and intermediate-range nuclear missiles be installed in its territory. They would be deployed surreptitiously in September and October, and the President of the United States wouldn't be told about them until November, when Khrushchev would be in Havana to sign a military agreement after the U.S. Congressional elections. Mikoyan raised objections to the idea, because he feared the United States would find out about the missile installations before Kennedy would be officially informed; he also thought that Fidel Castro wouldn't agree to the missiles because of the military and political risks implied by having atomic weapons in his country. That is what Sergo Mikoyan, private secretary and son of the Deputy Premier, recalled about the exchange.

There's another anecdote about when and where the idea was first broached; saying also that it was in April 1962, but that the place was different. Fedor Burlastky, who worked in the Central Committee on Khrushchev's team, said that Marshal Rodion Malinowsky, Soviet Minister of Defense, was in the Crimea with the Premier when he called Khrushchev's attention to the presence of U.S. Jupiter nuclear missiles on the horizon, in Turkish territory. He warned that the missiles could hit their targets in Soviet territory 10 minutes after being activated, whereas the Soviets' IBMs would need 25 minutes to reach their targets in the United States. As this account goes, Khrushchev pondered for a moment and then told Malinowsky that they could create a similar situation for the Americans by placing nuclear missiles in Cuba, "just over the horizon from the United States. The Americans, after all, had not asked Soviet permission."[1]

There is a third version, which Khrushchev included in his memoirs, published in the 1970s. Khrushchev recalled it was during his visit to Bulgaria on May 14-20, 1962, that he had the idea of proposing to Cuba that nuclear warhead missiles be installed there — secretly, because he thought that by the time the United States got around to asking questions, it would be too late for them to do anything.

So, there are three different stories concerning the birth of an idea which was officially declared to have been devised to help Cuba defend itself against attack by the United States. Later revelations about the military situation then existing between the Soviet Union and the United States and statements by participants in that process, lead to the conclusion that there was another purpose, of at least equal importance to the Soviet government — which was to strengthen its strategic position in regard to its adversary's nuclear superiority. The idea was never presented to Cuba in those terms, but the Cuban government accepted the missiles, not only because they would make a U.S. invasion less likely but also because it considered that they might aid the security of the socialist camp.

That was 1962, when the United States had 17 times as many nuclear weapons as the Soviet Union. Robert McNamara, Kennedy's Secretary of Defense, has stated that at the time of the October Missile

---

[1] Raymond Garthoff, *Reflections on the Cuban Missile Crisis (Revised edition)* (Washington, D.C.: The Bookings Institution, 1989), 12.

Crisis the United States had 5,000 strategic nuclear warheads, while the Soviet Union had only 300; the United States had 1,500 bombers based in various parts of the world, while the Soviets had fewer than 150. The United States had quite a considerable advantage.

The U.S. arsenal included 600 B-52 bombers, 400 of which had Standoff Hound Dog air-to-surface missiles; 700 B-47s; and 900 tankers for refueling on flights to the Soviet Union if necessary. The Soviet fleet of bombers consisted of 100 Bison heavy jets and 80 Bear heavy turbo-prop planes. The U.S. tactical forces included 2,500 fighter planes and 500 transport aircraft, augmented by 15 reserve troops carrier wings, 11 Air National Guard reconnaissance squadrons and 5 communication squadrons. In addition to Air Force strategic units, there were 16 U.S. Navy attack carriers, with more than 400 attack bombers stationed in the Atlantic, Pacific, Mediterranean and Caribbean.

The Soviets had a few short-range missile-firing submarines, none of which had more than 100 missiles, and none of the submarines were ever deployed close enough to the U.S. coasts to be within range; none were in the Atlantic or Pacific at the time. The Soviets had nothing comparable to the new Polaris submarines, each of which could launch 144 nuclear-tipped long-range missiles that could reach targets in the Soviet Union. The United States had 229 ICBMs, and the Soviet Union, only 44, of which only 20 were operational at the time, as Colonel General Dimitri A. Volkogonov, head of the Institute of Military History of the Soviet Union, testified in a meeting on the Missile Crisis that was held in Moscow in 1989.[2]

No statement has been made that indicates just when the Soviets realized what the strategic situation was, but the United States had confirmation of its quantitative superiority at least two years before the missiles were installed in Cuba. Havana had no idea about the relative strengths of the big powers, while Kennedy himself received no information about this state of affairs until after he had been elected President — that is, a year before the crisis, when Eisenhower, the outgoing President, authorized that he be informed about the discoveries the U-2s had made on their flights over the Soviet Union.[3]

It should be noted that Khrushchev was deliberately using rhetoric about the Soviet Union's nuclear clout in order to confuse a lot of people. For example, he told the editors of U.S. newspapers in a press conference on July 16, 1962, that the Soviet Union was turning

---

[2] Dino A. Brugioni, *Eyeball to Eyeball* (New York: Random House, 1991), 254 and 255.
[3] Brugioni, *Eyeball to Eyeball*, 54.

out missiles like sausages and that they could hit a fly out in space. On several occasions, Fidel Castro has said that if he had known of the United States' strategic lead over the Soviet Union, Cuba wouldn't have agreed to having the missiles and would have advised the Soviet government to be more prudent.

From an historical point of view, the basis of the crisis was directly related not to this nuclear arithmetic but to Washington's policy of blockading Cuba and to the threats of attack on the island that appeared imminent at the time. In any case, both the defense of Cuba and its revolution and the closing of the nuclear gap were powerful reasons for strengthening the island's military capability.

The United States harassed and harried Cuba on all fronts with subversion, the economic blockade, sabotage in Cuba's key production centers, numerous attempts to kill Fidel Castro and other leading Cuban revolutionaries, and growing threats of direct aggression by regular forces of the United States. That — nothing else — was the root of the dangerous confrontation, in which Cuba was a strategic objective. The Cuban revolution was the protagonist in a singular conflict, the real center of gravity for all of the forces that were involved. To examine that process objectively in all its stages, it is absolutely necessary to follow the main thread linking its episodes, from the outset to its final resolution.

The international situation at the time contained other trouble spots which exacerbated the differences that fanned the Cold War. At the beginning of 1962, Washington and London agreed to resume nuclear testing, which held back the negotiations on general and complete disarmament that were stagnating in various international agencies. Every time one of the big powers carried out any nuclear tests, there was a further move away from the goal of reaching an understanding on the reduction of mass means of destruction. It was a never-ending cycle that made it difficult to ease international tension.

In January 1962, the Soviets and Americans decided to resume their contacts to discuss their positions on Berlin, but an incident occurred in the corridor between West Berlin and the Federal Republic of Germany in February that set the talks back. Later, in April 1962, the dialogue got under way again, and an understanding was reached on the military missions stationed in the city. The advisability of holding a summit in Berlin began to be considered, but the British and Americans raised objections to this. In the merry-go-round of negotiations on Berlin that seemed to be in perpetual motion, the Soviet Union proposed in July that Allied troops in the western sector of Berlin be replaced by those of lesser NATO and Warsaw Pact countries, but no agreement was reached on this.

In Asia, the attention of both Washington and Moscow was focused on Laos, a tiny country where an internal struggle was being waged in which the ideological and military interests of the two big powers clashed. In Vietnam — and on a smaller scale Laos, as well — U.S. intervention was already casting an ominous shadow, that would extend over the entire world, with extremely dangerous implications.

In Africa, civil war continued in the Congo, with intervention by the United Nations, various colonialist powers and the Central Intelligence Agency.

However, it was the Caribbean — an area of legendary conflicts, a former prize in the colonialist dreams of the big European powers and now a veritable hunting preserve for the powerful imperialism that had arisen in the western hemisphere — that the circumstances combined giving birth to an unprecedented threat to world peace.

In spite of its small area, compared to the vast continents, the Caribbean has been of special historic significance. Ever since the early 1800s, high-ranking U.S. statesmen publicly proclaimed their hope of seizing Cuba, the largest island in the Antilles, and on the eve of the 20th century, when the United States was drawing up its imperialist policy and flexing its muscles, the Caribbean became the main ingredient in its strategy of expansion — and Cuba, its main prey. In 1962, it seemed as if all of the winds that had buffeted Cuba for centuries had joined together. The future of the world was at stake there. For the first time since the discovery of nuclear weapons, the world was on the brink of an epic, devastating confrontation of immense destructive consequences.

That was the international scene on to which the Cuban Missile Crisis burst, but the roots of the conflict had been manifest ever since the triumph of the Cuban revolution in 1959. The crisis wasn't produced through spontaneous combustion or by chance or whim. The seeds of the climax already existed, nurtured by a policy of extreme aggression that reached a critical point in 1962 and went beyond the limits of the arms race during the Cold War.

Cuba had thrown off its yoke as a U.S. protectorate and was standing up against U.S. hegemony in its immediate sphere of influence, ignoring all of the strictures that had prevailed until then and recovering its dream of becoming autonomous — a cherished dream since its people first took up arms against the Spanish colonial power. It wasn't only the Cuban people's socialist course — in which, of course, they were acting entirely within their rights — that accentuated the antagonism of the U.S. ruling classes, because Washington had expressed its bellicosity long before socialism was proclaimed.

Even before the 1959 revolution, in the period when the Batista dictatorship was plummeting toward its end, the United States had tried to keep the revolutionary forces from taking power. Then, in the first few months of 1959, when the revolutionary government was taking its first steps, Washington plotted to halt the social and economic changes that were transforming the Cuban scene. A group of high-ranking government officials headed by Vice-President Richard Nixon, J. Edgar Hoover (head of the Federal Bureau of Investigation), Arthur Gardner and Earl Smith (former U.S. ambassadors to Cuba who had protected their pal Batista),[4] and William Pawley (a notorious figure who worked for the CIA), offered Batista a guarantee that he could sit back and enjoy his wealth if he put a pro-Washington military junta in power and kept the insurrectional forces at bay. These conspirators worked in the White House, the CIA and Congress to sabotage the Cuban revolution while official spokesmen issued public statements making it appear that the United States was going along with the social justice measures in Havana.[5] The foundations that inexorably led to the 1962 Missile Crisis were established in early 1959.

Right from the start, U.S. hostility to the Cuban revolution took many forms. When Fidel Castro went to Washington in April 1959 in response to an invitation extended by the American Society of Newspaper Editors, President Eisenhower left the capital to avoid meeting with him — leaving Nixon to talk with him in the Capitol — even though his government maintained diplomatic relations with Havana.

The events that followed as a result of the revolution and Washington's reaction to it accelerated the breaking of Cuba's dependence on the United States. The Agrarian Reform Law of May 1959 was absolutely necessary for undertaking the country's development and was enacted under the old constitution and in exercise of the nation's sovereignty. Because it hurt the interests of the big U.S. landowners, it triggered new plans of subversion. In July 1959, the United States used a flimsy pretext to suspend Cuba's sugar quota on the U.S. market. That same month, on the instructions of the Treasury Department, U.S. companies cut off their shipments of oil to

---

[4] Richard Nixon, *Six Crises* (New York: Doubleday and Company, 1962), 352.
[5] John Dorshner and Robert Fabricio, *The Winds of December* (New York: Coward McCann and Geoghegan, 1980), 153 and 158.

Cuba. Several times the Cuban government proposed negotiating the differences that had arisen, but no agreement was ever reached. The United States was already determined to wipe out the revolution.

On March 17, 1960, Eisenhower ordered the CIA to train Cuban counterrevolutionaries in Guatemala so they could launch an invasion;[6] on October 27, he authorized the first U-2 spy flights over Cuba;[7] while the State Department sent diplomatic notes to Havana recognizing its right to expropriate property but demanding "fair and immediate" compensation, maintaining the fiction of normal official relations. Cuba proposed negotiating on an equal footing, with an open agenda. Finally, on January 3, 1961, a few days before Kennedy was inaugurated, Eisenhower broke off diplomatic relations with Cuba.

The actions of the Eisenhower administration were a foretaste of the almost hysterical response that occurred during the administration that followed it. Many subversive actions were carried out in 1959 and 1960: bombs were dropped, planes flew from Florida to engage in sabotage in Cuba, CIA agents stole ships and planes, a vicious hate campaign was launched against the revolution, diplomatic measures were taken to isolate Cuba, and trade restrictions were applied.

The Eisenhower and the Kennedy administrations carried out both clandestine and diplomatic anti-Cuba activities, with special emphasis on the latter in the Organization of American States (OAS), the traditional, meek tool of U.S. foreign policy. Pressure was quickly brought to bear on the foreign ministers of other Latin American governments to get them to join in the campaign against Cuba, and a foreign ministers' meeting was held in Santiago, Chile, eight months after the 1959 revolution to adopt resolutions to halt the changes that were being wrought in Cuba, setting precedents for tightening the blockade. A year later, in August 1960, another foreign ministers' meeting was held, this time in Costa Rica. While the State Department had limited its focus to the Caribbean basin in the first conference, increasing the tension around Cuba, in the second foreign ministers' conference it resorted to Cold War rhetoric, with a statement denouncing intervention or threats of intervention in the American republics by any power outside this hemisphere. Cuba was not named, but it was clear that the statement referred to the solidarity that the Soviet Union had extended to the Cuban people and the revolutionary government's acceptance of that support.

---

[6] Dwight D. Eisenhower, *The White House Years: Waging Peace 1956-1961* (New York: Doubleday, 1956), 533.
[7] Brugioni, *Eyeball to Eyeball*, 55.

Together with the diplomatic offensive, radio stations in the United States engaged in psychological warfare. Cuba waged a tireless struggle inside the OAS and the United Nations, defending itself against those attacks and denouncing the United States' illegal actions which violated the principles and charters of the two international organizations. The political atmosphere in the Caribbean became more heated than ever before, which endangered peace and security in the region and introduced a destabilizing factor in the world, triggering a series of events which led to the nuclear crisis two years later.

On the world agenda of controversial matters, the Cuban problem had special characteristics that set it apart from other conflicts. As I have already noted, the United States' antagonism was due to the fact that Cuba had taken an independent path — not Cuba's ties with the Soviet Union. Cuba's first agreements with the Soviet Union were signed in February 1960, and diplomatic relations between the two countries weren't established until May 7 that year.[8] The Cuban revolution was independent of the Cold War; it was a native product, whose roots went back to the first war of independence against Spanish colonialism, in the latter part of the 19th century. The close relations that were subsequently formed with the Soviet Union and the other socialist countries never changed that historical reality.

Among other things, the United States tried to disguise its contradictions with Cuba, claiming that it was not a bilateral conflict but rather between Havana and the other members of the "inter-American system." It tried to ensure the complicity of the other Latin American governments and presented the rest of the world with this distorted view of what was going on, to justify its aggressive policy. Thus, tiny Cuba was portrayed as a threat to the vast hemisphere of great valleys, lofty mountains, large rivers and infinite seas. Likewise, the United States' conflicts with Havana were woven into the fabric of its antagonism with the Soviet Union to intimidate third countries, especially in Latin America, where deep imperialist ideological penetration awoke fears of the specter of the Kremlin. The United States may also have hoped to pressure the Soviet Union to abandon its

---

[8] A Soviet mission visited Havana between October 5-14, 1942. Later, between September 17, 1942, and April 25, 1946, diplomatic relations were maintained at the embassy level, with Andrei Gromyko, the Soviet ambassador, living in Washington. Diplomatic representatives were exchanged in April 1946. On April 3, 1952, relations were broken off after Batista's coup. On January 10, 1959, the Soviet Union recognized the revolutionary government. In April 1960, the two governments agreed to exchange ambassadors. Relations were officially established in May 1960.

links with Cuba in exchange for improved relations with Latin America as a whole.

On January 20, 1961, an extremely cold day in Washington, John F. Kennedy moved into the White House. Eisenhower bequeathed him the plans for an invasion of Cuba by the forces that had been trained in Guatemala. It was an unexpected legacy, which the new President made use of three months later, before he had recovered from the fatigue of his electoral campaign and before he had become familiar with the reins of power. On his inauguration, he faced the burning responsibility of waging a war he had not even heard of prior to November 1960, a few days after his election. Cuba, of course, was clearly in the mind of the new president since it had been much debated in the electoral campaign against Nixon. The Democratic and Republican candidates had used all manner of demagogic weapons, each trying to outdo the other in condemning the Cuban revolution. Nixon had been cautious in proposing solutions for destroying it because, as a conspicuous promoter of the plans for military aggression, he didn't want to reveal the preparations that were already under way. Kennedy had gone to the other extreme. In a televised debate in September 1960, he said, "The forces fighting for freedom in exile and in the mountains of Cuba should be sustained and assisted."[9] Holier-than-thou, Nixon replied that, if his adversary's recommendations were followed, "we would lose all of our friends in Latin America, we would probably be condemned in the United Nations."[10] The Democratic candidate then changed his position and stated, "I have never advocated and I do not now advocate intervention in Cuba in violation of our treaty obligations."[11] It was an amazing about-face.

Those statements were given a lot of publicity in the United States and Latin America, and helped to create a warlike climate that made the relations of other Latin American countries with Cuba more tense and facilitated aggression. Public opinion was in this way conditioned to expect a violent outcome, no matter which candidate was elected.

April 1961. Acts of sabotage, strafing in the western and eastern parts of the island and finally the invasion at the Bay of Pigs completed the CIA plan, which Eisenhower had initiated and Kennedy carried out. Seventy-two hours later, it was all over. The revolutionary people

---

[9] Nixon, *Six Crises*, 353.
[10] Nixon, *Six Crises*, 355.
[11] *Speeches of Senator John F. Kennedy's Presidential Campaign of 1960* (Washington D.C.: U.S. Government Printing Office, 1961), 726.

won a rapid victory, and the humiliation to which Kennedy was subjected because of the defeat was a determining factor in his adoption of immediate measures against Cuba and in his promotion of plans of direct aggression using the regular forces of the United States. This in turn made it necessary for the Cuban government to strengthen the country's defenses and request Soviet assistance. Khrushchev's offer of nuclear missiles was a consequence of that request.

On August 4 and September 30, 1961, representatives of Cuba and the Soviet Union signed two agreements; in them, the Soviets pledged to supply military equipment to Cuba up through 1964. The pledge included armaments for the Army, Air Force and Navy — artillery of several kinds, tanks, armored cars, radio location stations and other means of communication, MiG-15 fighter planes, IL-28 bombers, MI-4 helicopters, cargo planes, airport equipment, torpedo boats and submarine chasers — and military specialists. That aid was essential for the country's defense.

Before the CIA invasion, Cuba hadn't been able to buy the weapons it needed to repulse an attack from abroad, because the United States sabotaged the efforts it made in Western Europe, especially in Belgium and Italy. Cuba's ability to confront the 1961 invasion was improved because the socialist countries — especially the Soviet Union — had sent some weapons to Cuba in the latter part of 1960: light weapons, artillery, mortars, tanks, self-propelled cannon and other supplies. As already noted, the more important agreements were signed after the attack.

The Bay of Pigs defeat meant a great loss of prestige for the Kennedy administration and undermined the President's authority. An acute U.S. observer of the era described what that failure meant to the U.S. President as follows:

It would seriously disturb the balance of the first two years of the Kennedy administration; it would almost surely necessitate a harder line both to prove to domestic critics that he was as tough-willed as the next man, and to prove to the Russians that despite the paramount foolishness of this adventure, his hand was strong and steady. By necessity now, an administration which had entered almost jaunty, sure of itself, a touch of aggressiveness and combativeness to it, a touch of wanting to ease tensions in the world, would now have to be more belligerent both for internal and external reasons, and it would not be for another 18 months, when the Kennedy administration had already deepened the involvement in Vietnam, that it would begin to retrieve a semblance of its earlier balance...

If anything, the Bay of Pigs had made the Kennedy administration acutely aware of its vulnerability and determined to show that it was worthy, that this was not a weak young President...[12]

When he decided to go ahead with the invasion, Kennedy placed too much confidence in the Pentagon hawks and CIA adventurers who assured him that the landing would immediately trigger a people's rebellion in Cuba. The bitter experience taught him that any military action against Cuba would have to be carried out by the armed forces of his country, and not by Cuban counterrevolutionaries, who had proved unequal to the task. That was a key factor for bringing the contingency plans for aggression up to date and developing an ambitious program of subversion, paving the way for a large-scale attack — which, as set forth in subsequently declassified U.S. documents, was to culminate in the overthrow of the Cuban government in October 1962, the month of the Missile Crisis.

U.S. domestic policy needs also helped to promote the projects for undermining the Cuban economy, fomenting disturbances and carrying out assassination attempts on the leaders of the revolution. Kennedy didn't want to present a vulnerable flank to the more reactionary forces in the Republican and Democratic parties. Both political organizations were working with an eye to the November 1962 congressional and gubernatorial elections, whose results would influence the 1964 presidential election, when Kennedy would stand for reelection. Khrushchev himself suggested keeping the presence of nuclear missiles in Cuba a secret until after the November election, presumably so as not to damage Kennedy's prospects.

Kennedy didn't have any rivals in the Democratic Party, and everything indicated that his Republican opponent would be New York Governor Nelson Rockefeller, though Senator Barry Goldwater, of the extreme right wing (who, in fact, became the Republican candidate after Kennedy was killed) also had considerable backing. With either of the two, Kennedy would have to defend himself against accusations that he had been weak and incompetent in failing to order an invasion with U.S. forces when the CIA-sponsored attackers were calling for direct intervention to save them from defeat at the Bay of Pigs.

---

[12] David Halberstam, *The Best and the Brightest* (Connecticut: Fawcett Crest Book, 1972), 84 and 92.

An enormous, overly-ambitious plot was designed. It linked the bureaucratic superstructure, particularly Robert Kennedy, to the elements that were in charge of implementing military and paramilitary plans, although the CIA evaded all supervision in some of the projects. At the same time, the State Department created conditions that were propitious to clandestine activities. One of the State Department's responsibilities was to encourage Latin American governments to break their ties with Cuba, and CIA agents collaborated in this, falsifying documents to place the Cuban government in a compromising situation and cause the breaking off of diplomatic and trade relations. In addition, the State Department bribed politicians, police, military officers and journalists to bring them into the plan.[13] Several Latin American countries broke off their relations with Cuba, placed obstacles in the way of travel to the island and supported the trade restriction measures in 1961 and 1962.

Since June 1961, when he had met with Khrushchev in Vienna, Kennedy hadn't hidden his frustration over what had happened with the invasion of Cuba. It was the first time that the two leaders had met, and Khrushchev came away from the meeting persuaded that Kennedy wanted to recover from the humiliating defeat by attacking Cuba with regular forces. The Soviets informed Fidel Castro of Khrushchev's impression of that meeting; they reported that Kennedy had seemed very hostile and had reminded the Premier that since the Soviets had solved the problem of Hungary in 1956, the Americans would have to solve the problem of Cuba.

Another indication of the plans of aggression that were being considered came in January 1962 when Alexei Adzhubei, editor of *Pravda* and Khrushchev's son-in-law, visited Kennedy in Washington; the U.S. President once again referred to the problem of Hungary. On a trip to Havana, Adzhubei told Fidel Castro about the conversation. Fidel Castro has said that after those talks Khrushchev seemed very worried and that the subject was mentioned frequently, before the idea of installing the missiles ever came up.

Washington's subversive program, called Operation Mongoose, was completed in November 1961. A high-level interdisciplinary group was created to supervise it. That body, the "Special Group (Augmented)," consisted of General Maxwell Taylor, McGeorge Bundy (special adviser to the President for National Security), CIA Director

---

[13] In his book *Inside the Company — CIA Diary*, Philip Agee tells of his experiences as a CIA agent in various Latin American countries, giving details about falsified documents and bribes.

John McCone, General Lyman Lemnitzer (head of the Joints Chiefs of Staff), Under Secretary of Defense Roswell Gilpatric, and Robert Kennedy, its main figure. Secretary of State Dean Rusk, Secretary of Defense Robert McNamara and high-ranking officials from other departments also took part in its deliberations, when this was considered necessary. Brigadier General Edward G. Lansdale, who had a lot of experience in adventures of this kind, headed Operation Mongoose. He had been in the Philippines in the 1950s to advise the government there in the struggle against the Huk guerrillas, and then worked for the CIA in Saigon during the war in Vietnam. A complementary operational unit, Task Force W, was also created, headed by CIA agent William King Harvey, a character whose record was filled with clandestine operations and who had been an FBI man before he was dismissed for drunkenness and joined the Agency. He was notorious for his histrionics and for always packing a pistol at meetings at the Agency's general headquarters.[14]

The Kennedy administration also tried to get the Latin American governments to convene another foreign ministers' conference with the purpose of imposing sanctions against Cuba — an action the Eisenhower administration hadn't taken. The idea of such a meeting was discussed in the OAS Council, and Mexico and Cuba pointed out the irregularity of the procedure that was being used to call the ministerial meeting. The United States had the votes, however, and a venue and date for the meeting were set: Punta del Este, Uruguay, in January 1962. Mexico and Cuba voted against the meeting, and Argentina, Bolivia, Brazil, Chile and Ecuador abstained.

The sanctions that Washington sought under the terms of the Rio Treaty included the breaking of diplomatic and trade relations, the interruption of communications and even the use of armed force. However, large and influential Latin American countries opposed this escalation, and a last-minute solution was found that satisfied the United States' desire to isolate Cuba as a prelude to aggression.

This compromise solution, which stated that a Marxist-Leninist regime was incompatible with the inter-American system, violated the OAS Charter — which did not allow the expulsion of any member, for whatever reason. Likewise, it went counter to the Charter of the United Nations — which prevailed over that of the OAS, a regional body of the United Nations — because the UN Charter opposed discrimination against any country for socioeconomic reasons. Moreover, the OAS was

---

14 Arthur M. Schlesinger, *Robert Kennedy and His Times* (New York: Ballantine Books, 1978), 514.

not able to adopt a restrictive coercive measure, as it did in Uruguay, without authorization from the Security Council of the United Nations. It is perfectly clear that the activities of a regional body must be compatible with the aims and principles of the United Nations, but this fact didn't bother Washington; it was a legal technicality that could be overlooked, since it had enough votes to impose its will. (The same countries that had abstained in the vote on holding the meeting, in addition to Mexico, abstained in the vote on this "solution.") Cuba later went to the UN Security Council, asking that it expose what the OAS had done, and requested an impartial ruling from the International Court of Justice on the legality of the resolution, but Washington engaged in more maneuvers and got a majority to keep the International Court of Justice from considering the matter.

Cuba's expulsion from the OAS was another indication that Havana was being cut off preparatory to more serious action, making it imperative to strengthen the country's defenses. The OAS resolution came nine months ahead of the last stage of Operation Mongoose and nine months, also, before the Missile Crisis.

The foreign ministers' conference resolution had another serious consequence, as well. The U.S. government used the resolution as a pretext for imposing a total blockade on trade with Cuba. In issuing Presidential Proclamation 3447 in early February 1962, a few days after Cuba was expelled from the OAS, Kennedy said he was basing his action on the decision made in Uruguay — even though no economic sanctions of any kind were adopted there. The U.S. proclamation banned imports of products of Cuban origin and all products imported from or through Cuba to the United States and ordered the Secretary of Commerce to continue to prohibit exports of any U.S. products to Cuba. Not satisfied with this, Kennedy sent Assistant Secretary of State Walt Rostow to Europe to try to get the U.S. allies in NATO to join the blockade of the Cuban revolution.

The offensive didn't stop there. The United States unilaterally rescinded Cuba's most favored nation status and preferential treatment, and the 1962 Foreign Aid Law stated that no assistance of any kind would be offered to the Cuban government or to any country that offered it help — which went beyond bilateral relations by punishing third parties that maintained links with Cuba. Cuba was to be given no assistance or quotas which authorized imports of Cuban sugar to the United States, nor any other benefits under any U.S. law.

On February 20, 1962, less than two weeks after Cuba's expulsion from the OAS, General Lansdale made public the project he had been working on ever since November, when the Executive formally created

Operation Mongoose. Only a few people knew about Project Cuba, as it was called, when it was submitted for approval. Lansdale recommended that knowledge of it be limited to Robert Kennedy, General Taylor, Dean Rusk, Ambassador Alexis Johnson, Richard Goodwin — these last three from the State Department — McNamara, Gilpatric, Generals Lemnitzer and Craig, the Director of the CIA, Richard Helms (the number two man in the CIA), Harvey (the head of Task Force W), and Edward R. Murrow and Donald Wilson (of the United States Information Agency).

Since January 1962, more than 5,000 counterrevolutionary actions had been carried out in Cuba, many of which consisted of acts of sabotage in key areas of the economy, such as the destruction of hundreds of thousands of hectares of sugarcane and warehouses filled with merchandise, attacks on cargo ships, the strafing of hotels near the coast and assassination attempts against government leaders.

Lansdale's plan called for actions to overthrow the Cuban government in four phases, between March and October 1962. The climax would be a people's uprising prepared by the CIA, followed by the military occupation of the country and the formation of a government put together in Washington.

Each phase consisted of several steps, which were linked together, including infiltration of agents, guerrilla bases — which the CIA was already supporting — strikes, open assistance from the United States if the new government controlled even only a part of the territory and psychological warfare. In March 1962, some directives for Operation Mongoose were drawn up, stating that internal and external resources should be used to the fullest, recognizing that final success required military intervention by the United States. In June, 12 infiltrations of Cuban territory were planned, using CIA agents. In July, the Department of Defense updated one of its contingency plans for an invasion and air attacks to support an internal revolt. According to a report submitted to the Special Group on July 25, 11 groups of CIA agents had been infiltrated to carry out acts of sabotage, conduct intelligence work and try to reorganize the groups of counter-revolutionaries who were operating in Cuba but were scattered and demoralized by the blows they had been dealt. Nearly all of their leaders had been arrested, and small groups that had penetrated into the country along the coast were being captured on almost a daily basis.

None of those setbacks had any effect on or perturbed General Lansdale, who kept on producing dozens of schemes "to get Castro."[15] His mind was bursting with ideas of all kinds. One of them deserves special attention because of its undeniable originality. It called for convincing Cuba's large Roman Catholic population "that the Second Coming was soon and that Christ would return in Cuba if the Cubans first got rid of Castro, the anti-Christ."[16] In other words, the head of the revolution would have to leave his homeland so Christ might enter it. In accord with this unusual plan, rumors were to be circulated that Christ would soon appear in Cuba, leading to a people's uprising. At that moment, U.S. Navy submarines would fill the night sky with fireworks in the form of tiny stars, which would be a sign to the "natives" that the Messiah was at their gates, and this would bring about the fall of the revolution. "Elimination by illumination," was how Walter Elder, Executive Assistant to the Director of the CIA, referred to this melodramatic stratagem.[17]

It was just one of the 33 proposals that were submitted to Kennedy as part of Operation Mongoose. The President, who was a Catholic of Irish descent, seems not to have believed that Christ would choose the Caribbean for His Second Coming, for he turned thumbs down on the idea. Instead, he supported the plan to "Exert all possible diplomatic, economic, psychological, and other pressures to overthrow the Castro-Communist regime, without overt employment of U.S. military."[18]

In the official jargon, this was Enlarged Variant B contained in National Security Action Memorandum 181 of August 23, 1962, which was signed by McGeorge Bundy as directed by the President.[19]

This scheme covered all possibilities. The bureaucratic ambiguities which filled the bulky file on the anti-Cuba conspiracy either hid or were explicit about the actions being devised, depending on what best suited the purposes of the plot. They included biological and chemical warfare to destroy the sugarcane, the gathering of intelligence data, infiltration of paramilitary troops, the forging of money and ration cards, attacks on refineries and the placing of explosives in stores and factories. The phrase "without overt employment of U.S. military" had

---

[15] John Ranelagh, *The Agency: The Rise and Decline of the CIA* (Britain: Sceptre, 1987), 386.

[16] Ranelagh, *The Agency*, 386.

[17] Ranelagh, *The Agency*, 386.

[18] *The Cuban Missile Crisis, 1962: A National Security Archive Document Reader.* Edited by Laurence Chang and Peter Kornbluh, (New York: The New Press, 1992), 47.

[19] *The Cuban Missile Crisis, 1962,* 61 and 62.

a hypocritical ring, in view of the Pentagon's contingency plans for an invasion, the directives that were announced in March, the military occupation if the rebellion were successful and the "last resort" — that everyone kept harping on — of using the Armed Forces at the end of all the stages that had been outlined. If it weren't necessary to send troops, planes and ships with flags flying, that step would be avoided, but if full military strength had to be employed to ensure the establishment of a stable government, it would be naive to think it wouldn't be done. Robert Kennedy stated this clearly in a meeting of the Special Group on January 19, 1962. He declared that Operation Mongoose had top priority for the government and that everything else was secondary. "No time, money, effort, or manpower is to be spared... Yesterday... the President indicated [to the Attorney General] that the final chapter had not been written — it's got to be done and will be done."[20]

Task Force W installed a colossal apparatus of espionage and subversion in Coral Gables, Florida, home of the University of Miami. Reports presented in the 1975 public hearings of the Church Committee of the Select Senate Committee on Intelligence Operations showed that of all CIA centers anywhere in the world, only its Langley headquarters had more resources and personnel. This center — JM/WAVE in the CIA argot — was one of the largest employers in the State of Florida.

In addition to generating its own operations, this center served as liaison with other CIA centers in Latin America in actions they undertook against Cuba. From 300 to 400 "case officers" of the Agency's clandestine services worked in the quiet academic environment of the university town. Each of those officers had from four to ten main agents — known as AMOTS — at their orders, and each of those main agents gave orders to some 10 to 30 regular agents, almost all of them Cuban counterrevolutionaries who lived in the United States. In her book that described the Center's structure,[21] Joan Didion commented that the arithmetic of the operation was impressive. Even if you took the lowest figures, with 300 "case officers," each of whom gave orders to four main agents, each of whom, in turn, gave orders to 10 regular agents, the total came to 12,000 regular agents. If you took the highest figures, the total came to 120,000 regular agents.

Fleets of small vessels and mother ships disguised as cargo vessels operated under the umbrella of the center. An unidentified CIA source

---

[20] Ranelagh, *The Agency*, 386.
[21] Joan Didion, *Miami* (New York: Simon and Schuster, 1987), 90 and 91.

described this fleet to the *Miami Herald* as the third largest armada in the entire western hemisphere.

Southern Air Transport, a plane company that the CIA bought in 1960, which was later financed by Actus Technology, Inc., was also assigned to the JM/WAVE unit, as was another CIA company called Pacific Corporation, funded with more than $16.7 million in loans from Air America, another CIA property, and another $6.6 million from Manufacturers Hanover Trust.

But that wasn't all. It had dozens of properties all over Miami, residential bungalows which it used as safe houses and coastal properties that served as anchoring places for hiding the vessels that engaged in operations in Cuban waters, infiltrating agents and transporting arms and explosives. Zenith Technological Services, the headquarters of JM/WAVE, had 54 other businesses that served as fronts for its clandestine activities and provided jobs and services for the center's operations, CIA-operated boat stores, CIA gun shops, CIA travel agencies, CIA real estate agencies and even a CIA detective agency.

What about the plans for assassinating Fidel Castro? Some of them, as revealed in the U.S. Senate investigations, were designed to be carried out by Mafia figures who had lost their gambling clubs in Cuba: Meyer Lansky, John Roselli, Sam Giancana, Santos Trafficante and less important figures. Examples of those assassination plans included soaking Fidel Castro's cigars with botulinum, a powerful poison that causes almost immediate death; putting poison pills in the Cuban leader's chocolate milkshakes in the Havana Libre Hotel; placing a seashell filled with explosives where he used to go swimming; and contaminating a diving suit with a fungus and another lethal agent that would cause a serious illness. The diving suit was to be given to Fidel Castro by James B. Donovan, who was negotiating for the release of the Bay of Pigs prisoners; Donovan wasn't to know that it was tampered with. The plan fell through, however, because Donovan bought another one.

Two accomplices in these schemes met bloody ends. Giancana was murdered in his Chicago home in 1975 while frying some sausages, shot seven times in the mouth and throat. And, in 1976, Roselli's body was discovered in an oil drum at the bottom of the sea near Miami Beach. (The CIA had intervened on Roselli's behalf with the U.S. Immigration and Naturalization Service in 1971 so he wouldn't be deported.)[22]

---

[22] Schlesinger, *Robert Kennedy*, 521.

The exact number of assassination attempts against Fidel Castro isn't known. The Cuban security services have captured many CIA agents who were infiltrated or were active on the island and have seized the weapons that were to have been used to assassinate him. Those assassination attempts have an important place in all the plots against the Cuban revolution.

2

Missiles and threats

On his return to Moscow, after visiting Bulgaria in May 1962, Foreign Minister Andrei Gromyko immediately told Khrushchev the idea of proposing to Cuba that atomic missiles be installed — which made Khrushchev think that it had already been discussed with the military chiefs. In fact, Marshal Rodion Malinowsky, Minister of Defense, had discussed the idea in a meeting in his ministry with Marshals Matviel Vasilievich Zakharov, head of the General Staff, and Sergei Biriuzov, head of the Strategic Missile Forces, and with Generals Vladimir Dimitrievich Ivanov, First Deputy to the General Staff, and Anatoli I. Gribkov, of the Main Operations Department. Later, the matter was submitted to the Presidium of the Central Committee of the Communist Party, which approved the proposal without any objections.

Once this had been done, there was the matter of presenting the proposal to the Cuban government. It was decided to call Alexander Alexeev, Counselor of the Soviet embassy in Havana, to Moscow. He had good relations with the Cuban leadership and as a TASS correspondent had been one of the first Soviets to have visited the island after the triumph of the revolution. As such, he had interviewed several important leaders, including Commanders Fidel Castro, Raúl Castro and Ernesto Guevara. Those meetings had taken place in October 1959. Among other things, they had discussed the sending of a Soviet trade and industrial exhibit which was then in Mexico to Cuba. In February 1960, Deputy Premier Anastas Mikoyan and Alexeev accompanied the exhibit.

Alexeev described his unexpected visit to Moscow as follows. The day after his arrival, he was invited to meet with the Premier, who told him he had decided to name him ambassador to Cuba. They were alone in Khrushchev's office in the Kremlin, and Alexeev stayed there for an hour, reporting to him on the situation in Cuba and answering his questions. Khrushchev spoke warmly of the Cuban leaders. He knew what was going on, not only because of the reports sent him by the embassy but also because he had met with many Soviets who had visited Cuba. Mikoyan in particular had praised the revolution. Khrushchev's daughter, Rada, and son-in-law, Adzhubei, had also filled him in. At the end of their talk, Khrushchev wished Alexeev success in his work and said that the Soviet government would do everything it could to help the Cuban people defend their achievements, but he didn't say anything about installing nuclear missiles. He said he would ask Alexeev to come back, with other leaders present.

Four days later, Alexeev was asked to return to the Kremlin. In addition to Khrushchev, also present were F.R. Kozlov, Second Secretary of the Central Committee; Mikoyan; Marshal Malinowsky; Gromyko; Marshal Biriuzov; and Sharaf Rashidov, alternate member of the Presidium. Alexeev repeated what he had told Khrushchev during his first visit. Khrushchev asked him many questions, especially regarding Cuba's defense capability and the decision to stand firm against U.S. pressures. Then he asked how he thought Fidel Castro would react if the Soviet government were to suggest that nuclear missiles be installed in Cuba. Alexeev was astonished and upset and said he doubted Castro would agree, since Cuba had already drawn up a strategy based on the Cuban people's willingness to fight and solidarity from world public opinion, especially in Latin America. At that point, Malinowsky interrupted, pointing out that the Spanish Republican government had accepted Soviet weapons during its struggle against the fascist forces.

Khrushchev then described Cuba's situation in detail and what advantages having the missiles would give it. He also said that, even if Fidel Castro didn't accept his offer, the Soviet Union would still give Cuba whatever help it needed, though he didn't think it would be enough to stop the aggressor. He added that he was sure, in view of the defeat the Americans had been dealt at the Bay of Pigs, that they would undertake an invasion of Cuba with their own armed forces; he said he had reliable reports to substantiate this prediction. He went on to say that the Soviets had to find an effective means to curb the United States so it wouldn't take that risky step. Khrushchev commented that statements in the United Nations in defense of Cuba weren't enough; the Americans had to be made to understand that, if they attacked Cuba, they would have to deal not only with Cuba's resistance but also with the Soviet Union's nuclear clout. "They must be made to pay through the nose for any warlike adventure against Cuba and, to some extent, be made to see that any threat to Cuba would mean [reciprocal action against] the United States... Logic shows that the only way to do this is to deploy our nuclear warheads in Cuban territory."[23]

Later on, Khrushchev said that since the Americans had encircled the Soviet Union with their military bases and missile installations they themselves should be made to see how it felt to live under a continual nuclear threat. He emphasized that the operation would have to be carried out with the utmost secrecy, to keep the weapons from being detected until they were ready for use. Above all, he added, it was necessary to avoid publicity in the tense period leading up to the November 6 congressional election in the United States. After the election, the agreement with the Cuban government — if the offer was accepted — could be made known. Cuba would be the center of attention in world politics, and it would be too late for Washington to act against it. Moreover, he said that the Soviets would be able to talk with the Americans on an equal footing. "To block the threats against Cuba, we must choose a method that doesn't lead to the unleashing of a thermonuclear war," Khrushchev said. He expressed his certainty that the Americans, who were pragmatic, wouldn't rush into taking a foolish risk, "just as we can't do anything now against the missiles that are deployed in Turkey, Italy and the Federal Republic of Germany aimed at the Soviet Union. Prudent politicians in the United States should think the same way we do now."[24]

After Khrushchev had spoken, it was decided to send a delegation to Cuba. It was to be composed of Rashidov, Marshal Biriuzov and Alexeev and was to discuss the Khrushchev's ideas with the Cuban government. Before leaving for Havana, the new ambassador was invited to the Premier's country home in Gorky. All the members of the Presidium who were in Moscow at the time were there, and Khrushchev repeated to them the ideas he had expressed in the earlier meeting.

---

[23] Cited in Sergio Del Valle, et al, *Peligros y principios* [Dangers and principles] (Havana: Editora Verde Olivo, 1992), 84-5.
[24] Alexander Alexeev, article written to be published on November 12 and 18, 1988. Author's files, translated from Spanish, 7-8.

The delegation went to Cuba posing as an agricultural mission, to keep the presence of such high-ranking military officers a secret. This was especially important in the case of Marshal Biriuzov, head of the Missile Forces, for knowledge of his presence would have aroused suspicion. Biriuzov traveled under the name of Engineer Petrov, and his true identity wasn't revealed until Alexeev informed Raúl Castro, Minister of the Cuban Revolutionary Armed Forces. Two nuclear ballistic missile specialists, Ushakov and Agueyev, accompanied the delegation.[25]

The group reached Havana on May 29, 1962, and made contact first with Raúl Castro and then with Prime Minister Fidel Castro. Even though Rashidov — who, in addition to being an alternate member of the Central Committee, was First Secretary of the Communist Party of the Soviet Union in Uzbekistan — headed the delegation, Biriuzov, who was the expert on missile matters, did a lot of the talking with Fidel Castro. Later, Fidel Castro described that meeting as follows:

> Biriuzov began by speaking not of missiles but of the international situation and of Cuba's situation in particular, the risks Cuba was running. At one point, he asked me what I thought was needed to keep the United States from invading, and I gave him an immediate reply. I said, "Well, if the United States were to understand that an invasion of Cuba would mean war with the Soviet Union, that would be the best way to keep it from invading Cuba"... He already had his ideas formulated, and he answered, "But, specifically, how? Something concrete must be done to indicate that." He had been assigned the mission of proposing that the strategic missiles be installed, and he may have been afraid that we wouldn't agree to it... We might have thought the missiles here could serve as grounds for criticism and campaigns against the [Cuban] revolution in Latin America, but we had no doubts when the idea of the missiles was broached. We thought they would help to consolidate the defensive power of the entire socialist camp... We didn't want to think just about our own problems. And, subsequently, they would mean our defense — subsequently! Then we asked some questions, such as what kind of missiles they were proposing and how many. We didn't have any practical knowledge about the matter. They told us there would be 42 missiles. Then we asked for time to call the [Cuban]

---

[25] Biriuzov was killed two years later in a plane accident just outside Belgrade while heading a delegation to the anniversary celebrations of the liberation of Yugoslavia.

leadership together and report to them; we said we would quickly do it. That's how it was; at the end of the meeting, we held a meeting with the comrades and analyzed the matter in these terms: the presence of the missiles would have certain connotations. We realized that the presence of those weapons would create great political tension, but we viewed the matter from the standpoint of our moral, political and internationalist duty, as we understood it.

When we met again with the Marshal and Rashidov, we told them that the leadership had agreed. We said, "If this will strengthen the socialist camp and also — and this is in second place — contribute to the defense of Cuba, we are willing to accept all of the missiles that may be necessary — even 1,000, if you want to send us so many." The decision was made.[26]

Fidel Castro made this statement in the January 1992 Havana meeting in which representatives of the three countries that had been involved in the Missile Crisis analyzed the conflict. He then went on to say:

If it had involved only the defense of Cuba, we wouldn't have agreed to having the nuclear missiles installed — not out of fear of the dangers that might ensue, but because of how they might harm the revolution, the image the [Cuban] revolution had in Latin America, since the installation of those weapons would turn Cuba into a Soviet military base, and that fact would take a high political toll. However, I believe that the installation of those missiles in Cuban territory strengthened the socialist camp and helped to even up the balance of power. I didn't discuss what I was thinking, whether what was being proposed would or wouldn't be helpful, because that would only have led to a decision not to accept the missiles, and I had noted that the offer hadn't been made in those terms, for those purposes. I had never viewed missiles as things that might someday be used against the United States in an unjustified attack, for a first strike. I remember that Khrushchev kept repeating that he would never launch a first nuclear strike. Really, deploying missiles in its territory wasn't absolutely necessary for Cuba's defense, because a military pact could have been entered into, and the Soviet Union could have said that an attack on Cuba was equivalent to an attack on the Soviet Union, as is stated in the pacts the United States has with

---

[26] Del Valle, *Peligros y principios*, 85-6.

practically everybody in the world, which are respected. Or a military agreement could have been entered into, and the purpose of Cuba's defense could have been served without the presence of the missiles.[27]

After their meeting with Fidel Castro, the members of the Soviet delegation had completed their work in Cuba, and they returned to Moscow. Some days later, Raúl Castro, Minister of the Revolutionary Armed Forces, went to the Soviet Union to formalize the agreement. He stayed there from July 3 through 16 and met several times with Khrushchev and with Marshals Malinowsky and Biriuzov to draft the agreement which set forth the conditions of the commitments. Sometimes two or three generals joined the discussions. Alexeev served as interpreter.

The top leaders of the two countries never signed the agreement, because the United States discovered the existence of the bases and the missiles, and events moved quickly. Raúl Castro and Malinowsky initialed the draft in Moscow, but when Fidel Castro read its text in Havana he made some modifications. The amendments he introduced were instructive regarding several aspects. First of all, they showed how scrupulously the Cuban revolution's principled positions were maintained in that document, which was so important in Cuba's international relations; they also demonstrated concern about clarifying any doubts that might arise regarding respect for the country's sovereignty and independence; and, lastly, they embodied the political vision held by the Cuban government since the beginning of the episode and that it maintained throughout the vicissitudes of the crisis, with a correct focus on the situation.

The document that was drawn up in Moscow was a rough draft that was subject to final approval by the two Heads of State, as is normal procedure in such cases. When Ambassador Alexeev brought the draft to Cuba in early August 1962 and gave it to Fidel Castro, the first thing the Cuban Prime Minister did was change the title of the document, which was originally the "Agreement between the Governments of the Republic of Cuba and the Soviet Union on Military Cooperation in the Defense of Cuba's National Territory." For the Cubans, that wasn't the purpose of the agreement — or, at least, not its only purpose. That was why the title was changed to include the defense of the Soviet Union, so that it became the "Agreement on

---

[27] Fidel Castro, Tripartite Conference on the Missile Crisis, Cuba, January 10, 1992. Translated from Spanish.

Cuban-Soviet Mutual Defense and Military Cooperation." Another important modification was to include a statement that the Armed Forces of the Soviet Union were legally bound to respect Cuba's sovereignty and legal system; therefore, they couldn't acquire rights of occupation or other rights unrelated to their functions. The agreement was to be in effect for five years, although either of the parties could end it with a year's advance notice to the other. It was also stipulated that when the troops withdrew, the installations that had been built would become the property of the Cuban government. Article 10 of the agreement stated that the Group of Soviet Troops would be directly under the Soviet government, which would cover the expenses of its men and provide all of the supplies the military contingent needed. For its part, the Cuban government would help in the deployment of those forces by offering them the facilities required where the different troops would be stationed. The text didn't mention what kind of weapons would be installed in Cuba.

Fidel Castro has said that the draft he received from Moscow was politically inconsistent in that no clear foundations were given. So he proposed Article 10 read as follows: "The two parties agree that the military units of each State will be under the command of their respective governments, and the two governments will determine in coordination the use of their corresponding forces for repelling foreign aggression and restoring peace."[28] Thus, there were to be two armies and two commands, and neither could give orders to the other.

Twice during the crisis (at the beginning and at the end) Cuba called for adhering to the principles of international law — which, among other things, strengthened its moral position. The first time was in the military agreement and the modifications of its text that were made. Two sovereign countries agreed to sign a pact in which both pledged to assume certain obligations, and the Soviet Union immediately accepted the changes that were made, to assign responsibilities and to add clarifications that weren't in the original text of the draft but which were incontestable, as Fidel Castro stated. The second time, at the end of the crisis, just after the Soviet Union decided to withdraw the missiles, was when Cuba outlined that guarantee in return for a U.S. promise not to invade Cuba. That guarantee, which I won't go into now (another chapter is devoted to them), required that the United States comply with its duty under international law by making its offer not to attack Cuba. Washington refused to accept the Cuban demands that were aimed at eradicating the causes of the

---

[28] Castro Fidel, *Tripartite Conference.*

conflict. Cuba proclaimed inalienable rights which, in fact, transcended the dispute between the two countries, since acceptance of them would have eased international tensions and removed an important threat to international peace and security. The U.S. refusal was in line with its aggressive policy toward Cuba and its decision to continue that aggression at all costs.

The saber-rattling campaign against Cuba was carried to unprecedented heights while the draft agreement was being examined. In Washington, demands were made in Congress for direct intervention by the Armed Forces; the Pentagon staged large-scale war games near the coasts of Cuba; clandestine operations were increased; the U.S. press stepped up its anti-Cuba campaign, infusing it with large doses of hysteria; Cuban airspace was violated every day; and the U.S. intelligence services carried their vigilance to an extreme, for rumors of unusual Soviet activity were rife. The Monroe Doctrine was even resurrected in a press conference given by Kennedy. That doctrine, which President James Monroe had proclaimed in 1823, stated that no European powers would be allowed to intervene in the western hemisphere in a manner prejudicial to the interests of the United States. When that obsolete doctrine was mentioned, the U.S. President said that it meant just as much to him as it had to Presidents Monroe and John Quincy Adams. Nevertheless, in the midst of the October crisis when the terms of a statement that Kennedy would make were being discussed and one of his collaborators mentioned the doctrine, Kennedy said, "What the hell is that?"[29] and ordered that no mention of it be made. In that meeting, the President declared that he didn't support an invasion of Cuba "for the time being," leaving in doubt just what he meant and saying that he didn't give the question of an invasion any special importance.

In fact, the doctrine played a key role as a pretext for actions against Cuba and hid the illegality of the measures that were taken. McGeorge Bundy highlighted its importance when, addressing a meeting that was held in Cambridge in 1987 to analyze the Missile Crisis, he said that the U.S. government's main problem was that it had repeatedly stated that the presence of "offensive" missiles in Cuba was unacceptable. Ever since the Monroe Doctrine had been proclaimed, "The United States has perceived a special interest in excluding

---

[29] James Blight and David Welch, *On the Brink* (New York: The Noonday Press, 1990), 363, note 40. The conference between academics and U.S. experts on the Missile Crisis was held on Hawk's Cay, Florida, in March 1987. Norbert Schlei, assistant to the Attorney General, was the collaborator who received Kennedy's reply.

European military power from the western hemisphere. This was a powerful fact of our political consciousness, regardless of the international legal question."[30] Clearly, the doctrine that the United States had proclaimed unilaterally and arbitrarily in 1823 still served as an excuse for eschewing international obligations and for ignoring the sovereign rights of other countries of the Americas if they got in Washington's way when it sought to further its own interests.

The press raised a hullabaloo, calling for the doctrine to be updated, and this was cited repeatedly in Congress, both in the legislators' speeches and in the texts of bills. The September 21, 1962, issue of *Time* magazine advocated a large-scale military attack on Cuba, citing the Monroe Doctrine. With gusto, it listed the names of political figures who had referred to it to justify an attack on the island. It said that Senator Kenneth Keating (R.) had stated on the floor of Congress that the Monroe Doctrine, the cornerstone of U.S. foreign policy, had been violated. In a letter to the President, Representative O. C. Fisher (D.) called for a naval blockade of Cuba, claiming that the Soviets were violating the Monroe Doctrine. Senator Thomas J. Dodd (D.) said that the United States should invoke the Monroe Doctrine to proclaim a total embargo against Cuba. Spruille Braden, former Assistant Secretary of State for Inter-American Affairs (and former ambassador to Cuba), called for a military invasion in the name of the Monroe Doctrine. Former President Harry S. Truman declared that the reason the United States had problems with Cuba was that Eisenhower had not had the guts to impose the Monroe Doctrine. Senator Strom Thurmond (D.) pointed out energetically that, in comments Kennedy had made about Cuba, he had reinterpreted the Monroe Doctrine with omissions. *Time* recalled that, in the Senate debate on the government's request for authorization to call up 15,000 members of the Reserves, the Republicans had presented amendments aimed at getting the Executive to "take action against Castro." Senator Prescott Bush (the father of former President George Bush and grandfather of President George W. Bush) presented an amendment stating that the United States had "the right and obligation" to attack Cuba. His amendment, Bush declared, would let the Soviet Union know that, far from dead, the Monroe Doctrine was still an integral part of U.S. foreign policy and would have to be imposed. Senator Jack Miller proposed an amendment that authorized and ordered the President to take whatever action might be necessary to prevent any violation of the Monroe Doctrine. This saber rattling reached its height before the

---

[30] Blight and Welch, *On the Brink*, 244.

missiles were discovered, and it formed part of the general plan for invasion that the Pentagon was meticulously preparing.[31]

An unprecedented joint meeting of the Senate Foreign Relations and Armed Forces Committees had been held on September 17, 1962. It lasted for five hours and was so well attended that there weren't enough chairs for all of the legislators and high-ranking government functionaries who showed up to discuss the situation in Cuba and examine the drafts that were presented. These drafts differed slightly in their wording but didn't stray from the main aim, which was to invoke the Monroe Doctrine in order to militarily attack Cuba, beginning with a naval blockade which would be binding on the U.S. allies in NATO. Secretary of State Dean Rusk and William P. Bundy, Assistant Secretary of Defense for International Security Affairs, were also present. Senator Richard B. Russell, head of the Armed Forces Committee, chaired the meeting.

While Congress and the President discussed the draft policy, a campaign to mold public opinion began with *Time* magazine publishing the draft documents.[32] All agreed that the Monroe Doctrine should be invoked, in the absence of anything else on which they could base their actions. It was said that one of the main sections of the doctrine — that the United States should not become involved in the conflicts of the European powers — had ceased to be applicable a long time previously, but that the part relating to the western hemisphere remained in effect. Mention was also made of recognizing a Cuban government in exile, but it was decided that this wasn't advisable for the moment, because the anti-Castro forces in the United States were divided.

The naval blockade had high priority in the discussion. Participants wondered if it would be a good idea to prevent British and Canadian ships from reaching Cuba. Dean Rusk commented that the use of force against ships en route to a blockaded country might be interpreted by the country whose ships were detained as a violent act preceding an act of war. One senator recalled that the British government had always been opposed to a naval blockade.

In view of all this, the Cuban government felt that it should take the initiative and not simply wait for things to get worse. It therefore asked the Soviet Union to make the military agreement public since

---

[31] *Time*, September 21, 1962.
[32] U.S. Declassified Documents on Cuba, 1961-1963 (on deposit at the National Security Archive, Washington, D.C.), 10-11.

Cuba, which was being threatened, had the right to strengthen its defenses and the Soviet Union had the right to offer assistance.

Commander Ernesto Che Guevara and Captain Emilio Aragonés Navarro, both members of the Political Bureau, were sent to the Soviet Union to suggest that the agreement — a copy of which, with the corrections made in Havana, they took with them — be made public. In an interview,[33] Aragonés stated that in their meeting with Khrushchev, the Soviet leader immediately accepted the modifications that had been made in the text of the document, but he didn't consider the time propitious for announcing the existence of the agreement, since Washington had not confirmed the rumors about the missiles' presence. Khrushchev felt that releasing the text at that moment would hurt Kennedy's electoral campaign. He added that, when the United States learned that the atomic missiles were positioned in Cuba, it would have no option but to accept the situation. Guevara and Aragonés had been told that the Soviets should make the final decision as to when to announce the agreement, because the Cubans had confidence in their experience.

After the talks, a communiqué was issued which stated that there had been an exchange of views relating to the threats made against Cuba by imperialist aggressors and that, because of those threats, the government of Cuba had appealed to the Soviet government, requesting weapons and the technical specialists required to train Cuban military personnel in their use. The communiqué went on to say that the Soviet government had taken the request into consideration and that an agreement had been reached on the problem. It added that, as long as those threats continued, the Republic of Cuba would be fully justified to take whatever measures it deemed necessary to guarantee its security and the defense of its sovereignty and independence and that all sincere friends of Cuba would be fully entitled to accede to those legitimate demands.

The communiqué didn't have as much legal or political value as the announcement of the military agreement would have had. The Cuban government had always wanted to make the agreement public. Subsequent revelations made by high-ranking functionaries in the Kennedy administration — who took part in the White House

---

[33] The interview was conducted on May 19, 1989, by Jim Blight, a researcher at the Foreign Policy Development Center of Brown University, and David Welch, a researcher at the Center for Science and International Questions of Harvard University.

discussions both before and during the negotiations on the crisis — endorsed Cuba's view on the need for a public agreement.

Abram Chayes, legal counsel to the State Department at the time, has since stated that his office always maintained that the installation of the nuclear missiles was legal. He said: "In fact, our legal problem was that their action was not illegal."[34] Theodore Sorensen, Kennedy's Special Adviser, and McGeorge Bundy, the President's Special Assistant for National Security, among Kennedy's closest collaborators, expressed views that if the Soviet Union had stated in the United Nations in September that it would defend Cuba with nuclear missiles, (Bundy) "It would have been a totally different situation" and (Sorensen) "[It] certainly would have made it more difficult for [the United States]" to act as it did.[35]

Fidel Castro had asked first Raúl Castro and then Guevara and Aragonés to question Khrushchev what he himself thought would happen if the operation was discovered before it was completed. Both times, Khrushchev replied that Castro shouldn't be worried, because, if the operation was discovered he would send the Baltic Fleet to Cuba. Commenting on this strange reply, Fidel Castro said, "We weren't thinking about the Baltic Fleet; we didn't think the Baltic Fleet could solve the problem. Rather, we were thinking about the Soviet determination and clout. The only thing that really protected us was the Soviet Union's global strength."[36]

Aragonés recalled that when Khrushchev told him and Guevara in front of Malinowsky that there wasn't any need to worry about a reaction by the United States, because he would send the Baltic Fleet should any problem arise, Guevara and he looked at each other and raised their eyebrows incredulously.

After Cuba had agreed, Khrushchev called a meeting in the Kremlin on July 7, attended by Marshal Malinowsky and the six members of the operational leadership of the Group of Soviet Troops Command which would be sent to Cuba. The Soviet Ministry of Defense was to start work immediately on maps of Cuba, to choose where to situate the missile groups and station the troops required for their security and defense. Major General Leonid S. Garbuz, who attended the meeting, recalled that Khrushchev underlined the importance of maintaining secrecy regarding the Group's deployment (especially that of the missile division) and the measures aimed at

---

[34] Blight and Welch, *On the Brink*, 40.
[35] Ibid., 247.
[36] Fidel Castro, Tripartite Conference, first session, 9 January, 1992.

quickly attaining high combat readiness. It was decided that the missile division should be sent first, followed by the general units. General Issa A. Pliiev (Pavlov) was named head of the Group.

Khrushchev said that the missiles were being installed to protect Cuba from attack. General Garbuz observed that, even though the Premier didn't include it in his aims, the better balance of strategic forces couldn't be ruled out, since Khrushchev also told the participants in the meeting that "the Central Committee has decided to make the United States' path more rocky by supplying missiles to Cuba... The missiles are just the beginning."[37] Garbuz understood this to mean that Khrushchev intended to do everything possible at once to achieve strategic force parity. Garbuz also pointed out that one of Khrushchev's concerns, which came out while he was addressing the mission, was to preserve peace and keep a nuclear war from being unleashed. He proposed to achieve this by extensively using camouflage and stationing the missile troops as quickly as possible so as to halt the unfavorable development of events and thus prevent the outbreak of a war.[38]

During the first phase of the operation there were no leaks; it was impressive how thousands of men, equipment, missiles, planes and torpedo boats were sent from Soviet ports to Cuba and then from their points of disembarkation in Cuba to their final destinations, without the intelligence services of the United States and its allies learning of the true dimensions and nature of the huge maneuver. The first troops arrived in August 1962, and the missiles in September, but it wasn't until mid-October that the U-2s photographed the missile installations, by which time some of them were already operational.

It isn't that U-2s didn't fly over Cuba during those months; they did, but before the missile installations were built. The United States realized there had been an increase in shipping to Cuba. British, German and other intelligence services reported to their Washington colleagues on what they had observed in Europe. They knew that the ships contained military equipment, and they suspected they had troops, as well, but they had no confirmation of this. The United States kept a close watch on Soviet merchant vessels during those months. Photos were taken from various vantage points — from shore, from other ships, and from aircraft flying at low, intermediate and high

---

[37] Del Valle, *Peligros y principios*, 90. General Garbuz was second in command of the troops for combat training and worked directly with the missile troops. He was interviewed in Havana in December 1989 and Moscow in 1990.
[38] Del Valle, *Peligros y principios*, 90.

altitudes. The photos taken by the Navy, Marines and Coast Guard included port, starboard, bow, stern and overhead views of the ships. Nothing remained unscrutinized. Vessels moving through the Bosphorus and Mediterranean were photographed by the Sixth Fleet and by squadrons stationed in Sicily and Spain. Once the Soviet ships passed Gibraltar or left the Baltic they were photographed by planes operating out of Kindley Naval Air Station in Bermuda and the naval air station in Jacksonville, Florida. As the ships approached Cuba they were spotted by the Marine photo squadron based at Guantánamo and by Coast Guard planes operating out of Miami.[39] But even that surveillance failed to reveal just what was going on. Doubts have been expressed about the way the installations, which the U-2s photographed half-way through October, were disguised. The photographs told the United States of the presence of nuclear weapons before the installations had been completed. Soviet military technicians said that the weapons could be hidden "in groves of palm trees" — a statement which General Gribkov later called "foolish." In the meeting held in Havana to analyze the crisis, Gribkov explained that, to install the missiles, they had to prepare the positions and command mechanisms, lay cables and pour the bases for the launching pads. And, of course, no palm trees could cover the missiles.

That wasn't the only thing preventing U-2 planes from taking photographs. The planes should have been kept from flying over the areas where the weapons had been placed. Fidel Castro commented about what the Cubans would have done if they had had command of the ground-to-air artillery: "I am sure the missiles could have been kept secret and the planes could have been shot down — as all the other U-2s that were making illegal flights had been... One question that might be asked is, why were the ground-to-air missiles here? What did they do? Why, after the ground-to-air missiles were emplaced, were the U-2s allowed to fly?... What would have happened if the U-2s hadn't passed overhead, if one had been shot down and it didn't take any pictures? If we had had those missiles and had been in on that operation, you may be sure that the U-2s wouldn't have flown over Cuba. What really happened is incomprehensible. That was a political, not a military mistake, because they undoubtedly had very strict orders; for political reasons, they must have had orders not to shoot at the U-2s... There were some mistaken political concepts as well as excessive pussyfooting. Because of Khrushchev's undeniable courage, I certainly don't hold it against him; rather, I feel grateful for his great

---

39 Brugioni, *Eyeball to Eyeball*, 72-3.

solidarity with our country and the help he gave us... I feel friendly toward him in spite of everything that might have happened."[40]

One precaution that the Soviets took was to name the operation after the Anadyr, a river in the northern part of the Soviet Union, in a very cold area. The troops were told they were going to participate in a strategic exercise there.

While Operation Anadyr was being carried out, the political situation between Cuba and the United States deteriorated. In late September 1962, the bill that had been drafted in the meeting on September 17 was presented in Congress. Its first paragraph began by referring to President James Monroe and his declaration that the United States would view any attempt by European powers to extend their system to any part of the western hemisphere as a threat to the peace and security of the United States. Immediately after that, it resolved that all means, including the use of armed force, be used to keep Cuba from extending its subversive or aggressive activities to any part of the hemisphere and from creating a military capability supported from abroad that would endanger the security of the United States. The Senate passed the bill on September 20 by a vote of 86 in favor and none opposed, and the House passed it on September 26 by a vote of 384 in favor and 7 opposed. The House had passed a Foreign Aid Bill a few days earlier with three amendments that suspended aid to any country that allowed its merchant vessels to be used to carry weapons and/or other merchandise to Cuba. On October 3, the foreign ministers of the other Latin American countries met in Washington, called there by the State Department. They issued a communiqué stating that the Soviet Union's intervention in Cuba endangered peace in the hemisphere. On October 4, Congress passed another resolution, recommending that the OAS adopt an agreement threatening Cuba with collective action if it continued to strengthen its military defenses. That same day, President Kennedy signed an executive order prohibiting the use of U.S. or foreign ships to carry merchandise between the Soviet Union and Cuba. U.S. ports were being closed to ships of any flag that carried military equipment to Cuba and to any ship that carried merchandise from "communist countries" to Cuba; in addition, the United States penalized foreign shipping companies that provided ships for trade between "communist countries" and Cuba and prohibited U.S. ships and ships owned by U.S. citizens from engaging in any kind of trade with Cuba.

---

[40] Fidel Castro, Tripartite Conference, first session, 9 January, 1992, 73.

On September 29, the Council of Ministers of Cuba replied to Washington's Joint Resolution of Congress. The Cuban statement listed the acts of aggression that the United States had carried out against Cuba and declared that, in view of Cuba's strict observance of the sovereignty of the other American countries, the imputation implicit in the Joint Resolution was both false and base. It further declared that Cuba would never engage in aggressive or subversive activities aimed at extending its sphere of influence to any other country in the hemisphere, nor would it ever use its legitimate means of military defense for aggressive purposes that would endanger the security of the United States. It said that while efforts were being made to present Cuba as a threat to the security of the United States and to other countries in the hemisphere, the government of the United States had resorted to all manner of means to overthrow the revolutionary government and destroy the political, economic and social order which the Cuban people were creating, availing themselves of the powers inherent in their self-determination, independence and sovereignty.

It pointed out that the government of the United States was at that moment pressuring such countries as England, Norway and Greece, for which shipping was essential, trying to keep their vessels from carrying merchandise (including foodstuffs and medicines) to Cuba. It had already managed to get the West German government to issue a prohibition of this kind. The document went on to say that if the United States would provide Cuba with effective and satisfactory guarantees to respect Cuba's territorial integrity and cease its own subversive and counterrevolutionary activities, Cuba wouldn't have to strengthen its defenses, "It wouldn't even need an army," and all of those resources would instead be used to promote the country's economic and cultural development. It added that Cuba had always been willing to discuss easing tensions and improving relations with the government of the United States if Washington would reciprocate this attitude. It went on to say that Cuba would have been able to pay compensation to U.S. citizens and companies that had been adversely affected by the revolution's laws if it hadn't been for the acts of economic aggression; and if the U.S. government had been willing to negotiate on a basis of respect for the Cuban people's wishes, honor and sovereignty.

The clamoring from Congress, the White House's threats and the saber rattling in the U.S. press weren't the only dangers threatening Cuba: ships, cannon and planes were mobilized near its coasts in war games that served as rehearsals for an invasion and as tools of intimidation which might be used, if the opportunity arose, for a surprise landing.

Before it had even occurred to Nikita Khrushchev to install nuclear missiles in Cuba, several military maneuvers had been carried out, one of them a large-scale action on the eastern seaboard of the United States between Norfolk, Virginia and Charleston, South Carolina. Eighty-three ships, 300 fighter planes and 40,000 men took part in that maneuver, which was held between April 19 and May 11, 1962. It was called Operation Quick Kick, and President Kennedy observed it from on board the aircraft carrier *Enterprise*.

Operation Whip Lash, in which several branches of the Armed Forces took part, was staged from May 8 through 18 to test the efficacy of one of the contingency plans for an invasion of Cuba, and preparations were completed for another military exercise in the Caribbean, a paratrooper attack called Jupiter Springs.

At 6:00 on the morning of July 24, some 30 U.S. Delta planes flew at a high altitude in fighter formation close to the town of Caimanera, near the Guantánamo Naval Base, dropping explosives on targets in the base and causing tremors in the town, which alarmed its inhabitants. Four days later, a Pentagon spokesman announced in Washington that the United States had decided to accept Cuban "refugees" in the Armed Forces of the United States and that they would be treated like any other recruits in terms of pay and other details. Doctors and dentists would be given officers' rank. Without anybody's asking, the spokesman went on to say that this wasn't a special force for invading Cuba.

August 1962. The U.S. Strike Command (USSTRICOM), supported by the Military Air Transport Service (MATS), carried out Swift Strike, an exercise in North and South Carolina. This was the first time that a conventional limited war was simulated. Four Army divisions, six squadrons of tactical fighter planes and two squadrons of tactical reconnaissance planes took part in the operation — 70,000 men in all. On September 7, the Tactical Air Command was ordered to form a work group to draw up a plan that would coordinate an airborne assault on Cuba with subsequent amphibious and paratrooper landings. That same day, President Kennedy asked Congress for authorization to call up 150,000 members of the Reserves. On September 18, Tactical Air Command aircraft began training to back up a contingency plan for bombing Cuba — known as OPLAN 312. On October 2, the Atlantic Command carried out Blue Waters, an exercise near Puerto Rico that lasted four days and whose purpose was to test the command and control procedures for a military operation in which the Army, Navy and Air Force were involved.[41] Recalling the Missile Crisis several years later, Admiral Robert L. Dennison, Commander of the Atlantic Fleet, stated that, two weeks before the ballistic missiles were discovered, orders had been given to prepare an air attack on Cuba under OPLAN 312 for a maximum alert on October 20. On October 6, Dennison received a memo from the Secretary of Defense informing him that the Joint Chiefs of Staff ordered him to begin carrying out "directives 314 and/or 316" – the ones referring to the invasion of Cuba. According to the chronology prepared by the National Security Archives in Washington, the Joint Chiefs of Staff informed the Atlantic Command on October 8 that the British government had secretly acceded to the U.S. request to proceed with pre-positioning of supplies and equipment on Mayaguana island, in the Bahamas, stipulating that the agreement couldn't be put in writing and that the installations couldn't be activated without the prior consent of London.[42]

The war games that were carried out starting in April must have been planned long before they took place, and one of the most important and dangerous ones from Cuba's point of view was scheduled for October 15. It never took place, because the nuclear missiles were discovered the day before, even though Kennedy made no public announcement to this effect. In any case, the discovery was used in part to cover up the deployment of troops and equipment near Cuba. The war games that had been held to display U.S. military clout left no doubt that they were a serious rehearsal for an attack on Cuba. They were conducted as an attack on Vieques Island, next to Puerto Rico – which, in the Pentagon plan, was turned into a fictitious "Republic of Vieques" with a dictator named ORTSAC (Castro spelled backwards), who was to be eliminated. Not much of an effort was required to get the point. The large-scale amphibious operation, Phibriglex-62, was to be two weeks long, with 20,000 sailors and 4,000 Marines taking part.[43] It shouldn't be forgotten that the final phase of Operation Mongoose called for a military attack on Cuba in October 1962, when it was thought that a people's rebellion would take place.

Robert McNamara, Secretary of Defense in the Kennedy administration, declared on two occasions that the United States never intended to invade Cuba. The first time was in the meeting held in

---

[41] *The Cuban Missile Crisis, 1962: A Chronology,* (Washington D.C.: The National Security Archive, 1990), 45, 48, 50, 52.
[42] Ibid., 52.
[43] Ibid., 54.

Moscow in 1989 in which Cubans, Soviets and Americans analyzed the lessons to be drawn from the Missile Crisis; the second was in a similar meeting held in Havana in 1992, in which Fidel Castro participated. McNamara emphatically denied that the United States had ever thought of ordering an invasion of Cuba before the nuclear missiles were discovered, but he acknowledged that, if he had been a Cuban, he would have thought otherwise: "If I was a Cuban and read the evidence of covert American action against their government, I would be quite ready to believe that the United States intended to mount an invasion."[44] McNamara insisted that despite the preparation of military contingencies in October 1962, the Kennedy administration did not intend to invade Cuba, by which he meant that no political decision to invade Cuba had been taken, and no serious discussions to consider such an operation had taken place among senior policymakers.

One of Kennedy's closest collaborators, Press Secretary Pierre Salinger, didn't believe what McNamara said. In an article published in the *International Herald Tribune* on February 6, 1989, commenting on the Moscow meeting — a meeting which Salinger also attended — the former White House spokesman wrote:

> To my disappointment, however, some of the participants seemed to judge the events of 1962 from the perspective of the cooled political climate of 1989 détente. It seems clear, for instance, that the Kennedy administration, under heavy political pressures, was indeed planning to invade Cuba in the fall of 1962, and that the Kremlin sent the missiles to Cuba to forestall an attack. But Robert McNamara, who was John Kennedy's defense secretary, denied that Washington had any such plans. While the conference helped fill many gaps in the record, some questions remain. One major one is whether the United States did not in some sense provoke a confrontation by planning a second invasion of Cuba, even after the embarrassing Bay of Pigs disaster in 1961.
>
> I have a lot of respect for Mr. McNamara. But his insistence that the United States never intended to invade Cuba, either before or during the crisis, flies in the face of the facts.[45]

Unquestionably, the facts spelled aggression. The Pentagon's contingency plans linked to the CIA's subversive operations; the

---

44 Robert McNamara, Tripartite Conference, 9 January, 1992, 9-10.
45 Pierre Salinger, "Kennedy and Cuba: The pressure to invade was fierce", *International Herald Tribune*, February 6, 1989.

economic blockade; the diplomatic maneuvering to isolate Cuba and the press campaign of vilification, had nothing to do with the war games that the military carried out on their bases to become more adept in handling the complicated mechanisms of military operations. The plans against Cuba were never filed away; rather, they were constantly updated. In October 1961, President Kennedy had ordered the Department of Defense to prepare secret plans for invading Cuba, with an air attack as an alternative; that decision was made a year before the missiles were placed in Cuba. That instruction also marked the starting point for the large-scale war games.[46]

In that climate of violence, Osvaldo Dorticós, President of the Republic of Cuba, addressed the General Assembly of the United Nations on October 8, presenting a message of peace to which Washington turned a deaf ear. He repeated what the Council of Ministers of Cuba had stated on September 29, saying:

> I declare here solemnly that, if the United States would guarantee by word and by deed that it wouldn't engage in any acts of aggression against my country, we would need neither our weapons nor our army. We want peace, and we are striving to create peace. Moreover, we are not obliged to give the U.S. Congress an account of what we do to defend our territorial integrity. We are arming ourselves in the way we believe necessary to defend our nation — not attack anybody. We don't have to give an account to any foreign Congress on that score. As long as the tragic circumstances require it, we will continue to strengthen our military defenses; if anyone attacks us, they will come up against the strength of our resistance, which consists of both weapons and patriotism.[47]

Turning to the U.S. delegation — Ambassador Adlai Stevenson was in his seat — Dorticós said that this was the moment for the United States to correct the Cuban fears of an invasion:

> I urge the head of the delegation of the United States in this assembly to offer full guarantees here that his government does not intend to attack Cuba. I urge him to offer those guarantees not only in words but above all in deeds. The government and people

---

[46] Nathan James, *The Cuban Missile Crisis Revisited* (New York: St. Martin's Press, 1992), Raymond Garthoff essay, "The Cuban Missile Crisis: An overview," 43.
[47] Osvaldo Dorticós, UN document, translated from Spanish.

of Cuba are fully convinced that a military attack by the government of the United States is imminent. When a small country such as mine feels threatened, a country of 6 million inhabitants just 90 miles from the United States, it has no reason for rejecting spontaneous assistance that is offered to it — no matter whether it comes from Queen Elizabeth of England, the Emperor of Japan, President Kubistchek [of Brazil] or anyone else — because the peoples' right to life is above all other considerations. My country stands alone in this hemisphere. I am filled with grief in saying this, because Cuba is a part of the Americas; Cuba is an essentially American country; and Cuba gave birth to José Martí, the only real equal Simón Bolívar has ever had in Our America.[48]

While Dorticós was speaking in the United Nations, the U.S. Congress passed another law which stated that the United States would withdraw all military and economic aid from any country which "sells, furnishes, or permits any ship under its registry to trade with Cuba so long as its governed by the Castro regime."[49] Several Western countries protested against that legislation, which extended U.S. jurisdiction extraterritorially to third countries. On October 19, in a letter to the UN Secretary-General, the Cuban government cited a large number of attacks against Cuban territory.

---

[48] Ibid.
[49] *The Cuban Missile Crisis, 1962: A Chronology*, 53.

3

The missile gap and discovery

The Nuclear Age was born among retorts, test tubes, reactors and cyclotrons in an inarticulate way. Prior to and during World War II, scientists working either on their own or as part of a team set about deciphering the mysteries of the atom. In the hushed atmosphere of British universities, at the College de France, at New York's Columbia University, in Chicago, in the Physiotechnic Institute of Leningrad,[50] in Sweden, Berlin, Denmark and in small laboratories in Warsaw, scientists from a wide variety of backgrounds, many of them refugees from Nazi fascism, made discoveries that later assisted the United States to manufacture the atom bomb. What began as a matter of scientific curiosity wound up being the most powerful, destructive and terrifying weapon known to humanity. It's military use in this period has had a very important political influence on international relations in the last 50 years.

---

[50] On Sunday, June 22, 1941, when Nazi troops invaded the Soviet Union, a short note appeared on the last page of *Pravda* reporting that the first cyclotron for experimenting with atomic fission had just been built on the grounds of the Physiotechnic Institute of the Academy of Sciences in Lesnoe, near Leningrad. I have taken this information from *L'Armee Rouge Assasinè* [The Red Army assassinated], by Alexandr Nekritch, (Paris: Bernard Grasset Publishers, 1968), 208 and 209. The information had already been published in Moscow in 1965 under the title: *1941, 22 Iyounia* [June 22, 1941].

In no other period of history had there been a confrontation between two adversaries with the means to destroy each other and to wipe out most of the world — destruction on an inconceivable scale. Nor had there ever been this phenomenon of such a "hot" conflict between enemies with irreconcilable ideologies who didn't exchange a single shot. But, in 1962, the world was very close to catastrophe. That year, the arms race was at its height and was the focal point of the so-called Cold War. The two powers with the largest nuclear arsenals were competing for superiority in means of mass destruction.

The two U.S. bombs that were dropped on the Japanese cities of Hiroshima and Nagasaki in August 1945 opened the door to nuclear rivalry. Subsequent events seemed like something out of a movie. In July 1949, the Soviet Union exploded its first atom bomb; in 1952, the United States exploded its first hydrogen bomb and the United Kingdom made its debut with its first atom bomb. In August 1953, six months after Stalin's death, the Soviet Union exploded its first thermonuclear bomb. In 1957, the Soviets put the first satellite into space and tested their first ICBMs. That same year, the United Kingdom exploded a hydrogen bomb. In 1958, the United States sent its first satellite into orbit, and the next year a Soviet rocket reached the moon. In February 1960, France exploded its first atom bomb; China exploded its first nuclear bomb in October 1964. At the same time, one round of disarmament negotiations after another failed, and talks for ending nuclear testing fared no better.

In 1962, Cuba became involved in this touchy situation when Soviet nuclear ballistic missiles with a range of 2,000 kilometers were installed on the island, and others with a radius of action of 4,600 kilometers were en route to Cuba on Soviet ships. These last, however, never reached Cuba: when the ships carrying them were near the Azores, the Soviet government ordered them to return to their ports of origin, because the United States had found out about the operation and imposed a naval blockade.

In 1961, U.S. spokesmen announced that the United States had achieved nuclear superiority over the Soviet Union. Up until then, nobody had known which of the two powers was ahead, and the question remained shrouded in uncertainty even then. There wasn't any way to know for sure, since the real data were closely-guarded secrets, both in Moscow and in Washington. However, the Soviets' decision to send missiles to Cuba led many to think that the Soviet Union wanted to even up the balance of power. Up until 1961, it was generally assumed in the United States that there was a "missile gap" between the two countries, with the Soviet Union having the advantage — or, at least, with each just as capable as the other of causing devastating damage to its adversary. What each of the rivals most feared was that the other might launch a first nuclear strike against its vital targets.

The polemic on the "missile gap" began in the United States in August 1957 when the Soviet Union successfully launched an ICBM for the first time and the United States was faced with one failure after another that same year. On five occasions, it failed to launch its missiles: four intermediate and one intercontinental. Then the Soviet Union shot *Sputnik* into space and placed a dog in orbit. Later, millions of television viewers watched another U.S. failed attempt to launch a satellite when it rose a few feet above the ground and blew up. Alarm spread, both in official circles and in public opinion, for the press publicly announced that the United States had fallen behind its principal enemy, and sectors in the main political parties played on this to serve their own interests. The Democrats — especially John F. Kennedy, who was already looking ahead to the presidential nomination — attacked the Republican administration for letting the Soviet Union get ahead in the arms race. Officers of the intelligence bodies even provided Democratic senators and journalists with secret reports which predicted that the gap did, indeed, exist; they did this to force the U.S. government to increase its defense appropriations.[51] Later, the question became one of the main issues in Kennedy's and Nixon's presidential campaigns, along with the problem of Cuba. It wasn't until a few days after Kennedy's election that the Eisenhower administration told him the facts about the strategic nuclear weapons situation between the two countries. The other surprise the President-elect was given was the news that the Central Intelligence Agency already had an invasion of Cuba ready to roll.

In October 1961, Kennedy decided to state publicly that his country had a greater strategic nuclear capability than the Soviet Union. This was a year before the Soviet leaders proposed to Cuba that medium- and intermediate-range ballistic missiles be placed in its territory. Deputy Secretary of Defense Roswell L. Gilpatric was to give an address at a businessmen's meeting in Hot Springs, Virginia, and the President asked him to use the occasion to reveal the truth about U.S. nuclear clout. The Deputy Secretary complied by saying:

---

[51] Roger Hilsman, *To Move a Nation* (New York: Doubleday and Co, 1967), 10.

This nation has a nuclear retaliatory force of such lethal power that an enemy move which brought it into play would be an act of self-destruction on its part.

The United States has today hundreds of manned inter-continental bombers... six Polaris submarines at sea, carrying a total of 96 missiles, and dozens of intercontinental ballistic missiles. Our carrier strike forces and land-based theater forces could deliver additional hundreds of megatons. The total number of our nuclear delivery vehicles... is in the tens of thousands, and, of course, we have more than one warhead for each vehicle.[52]

The 22nd Congress of the Communist Party was in session in Moscow, and in one of his addresses to the delegates Khrushchev referred to the United States' most recent acts of intervention in Lebanon, Laos and Jordan; the Bay of Pigs invasion in Cuba; the tensions it had created in Taiwan; and the Berlin crisis. Khrushchev said that the U.S. allies in NATO were threatening to resort to arms if the Soviet Union signed a peace treaty with Germany "to normalize the situation in West Berlin," and he announced a series of measures in view of the dangerous course of international events. The Soviet government would suspend the reduction of its armed forces (which it had decided in 1961), increase its defense budget, postpone transferring soldiers to the reserves and resume its nuclear tests with more powerful weapons. Later, he took the floor again and said that the struggle for general and complete disarmament was one of the pillars of the Soviet Communist Party's foreign policy, in accord with the principles of peaceful coexistence. "The stockpiling of weapons that is taking place in the atmosphere of the Cold War and warmongering hysteria," he commented, "leads to disastrous consequences. It takes only one addle-brained officer on guard to lose his nerve, something that happens, to push the button somewhere in the West and inflict tragedy on all the peoples of the world."[53]

Minister of Defense Marshal Malinowsky gave a more direct reply in the CPSU Congress to Washington's statements. Forty-eight hours after Gilpatric's speech in Hot Springs, Malinowsky stated that, with the approval of President Kennedy, the U.S. Deputy Secretary of Defense was "brandishing the power of the United States, threatening

[52] Michael Beschloss, *The Crisis Years: Kennedy and Khrushchev, 1960-1963* (Edward Burlingame Books, 1991), 330.
[53] N.S. Khrushchev, Speech on the 22nd Party Congress of the Soviet Union, author's files. Translated from Spanish.

us with force." He added that, "If war is not avoided in the future, it will be unprecedented in its destruction, causing the deaths of hundreds of millions of people and turning entire countries into lifeless deserts covered with ashes." At the end of his address, he warned that the Soviet Union had satisfactorily solved the problem of how to shoot down missiles in flight.

The polemic between the two big military powers continued with a sharp tone throughout that year and in the next took on extraordinary proportions, because discussions centered more on Washington's war against Cuba. In the second quarter of 1962, the Soviet Union proposed that Cuba allow atomic missiles to be emplaced in its territory, and the year ended closer to a nuclear conflict than ever before in the tense history of the Cold War. The 85 merchant vessels filled with Soviet troops that had left from seven different ports on the Baltic, Barents, White, North and Black Seas began arriving in Cuba in the first few days in August and unloaded the military personnel and then the rockets and the rest of the war materiel in eastern, central and western Cuba. It took 185 crossings to complete that phase of the operation — the largest operation the Soviet Union had ever carried out. The operational group, headed by General Pliiev, had been in Cuba since the previous month. The first R-12 rockets (SS-4s in U.S. terminology) arrived on September 15, and the nuclear warheads, on October 4.

The Group of Soviet Troops consisted of a missile division with five regiments — two of intermediate-range ballistic missiles and three of medium-range missiles, which were the only ones that arrived — four motorized infantry regiments, three of which had tactical nuclear missiles added; two more short-range ballistic missile regiments; two antiaircraft missile divisions; several combat support units, including a communications regiment, six independent battalions, two tank battalions, one battalion of sappers, a reconnaissance battalion, a radio battalion and a short-wave battalion; and an independent 10-mm. antiaircraft artillery group.

The air force consisted of a regiment of fighter planes with 40 MiG-21s, six MiG-15s and one MiG-17; a regiment of IL-28 light bombers; a regiment of 33 MI-4 helicopters; and a squadron of transport planes.

The naval forces had a brigade of missile-launching vessels consisting of three squadrons, each of which had four small ships, and a regiment of ground-to-sea missiles. Seven submarines, each of which had three R-13 missiles and four torpedoes, patrolled Cuba's coasts.[54]

When Kennedy announced on October 22 that atomic missiles had been discovered in Cuba, the launching pads for two regiments had already been completed, and work on a third was in its final stages (it was finished on October 25), though the nuclear warheads were never installed, nor were the liquid fuel and oxidizing agents ever prepared.

The negotiations between Khrushchev and Kennedy are described in the next chapter. To understand the role of the time factor in the negotiations, it should be kept in mind that the Soviet military experts had allowed two and a half hours for placing the R-2 missile systems in combat readiness: two hours and ten minutes for mounting the nuclear warheads on the missiles and placing the missiles on their launching pads and from 16 to 30 minutes for adding fuel and oxidizing agents, and programming the range data. Plans existed for building 24 launching pads for the R-12s and 16 for the R-14s (SS-5s), for a total of 60 missiles that could hit targets anywhere in the continental United States.[55]

The tactical nuclear missiles had a range of 60 kilometers, and the heads of the Soviet troops who were in Cuba — 42,000 men — could order them fired without asking for instructions from Moscow, as was required for using the strategic weapons. Their function was to repel an invasion. The members of the U.S. delegation to the 1992 Havana meeting were surprised to learn this.

According to General Gribkov of the Main Operations Department, the groups of tactical missiles had six launching pads for nine missiles with nuclear warheads, but Lieutenant General Belodorodov, who also participated in Operation Anadyr, said that the groups had 24 missiles with conventional warheads and 12 with 3-kiloton nuclear warheads.

In the 1992 Havana meeting, Fidel Castro stated that he thought there had been more tactical nuclear weapons. He said that Cuba could have been defended with tactical weapons, which would not have created an international incident, as would have been the case with the use of the strategic weapons. "Nobody could have said they posed a threat to the United States," said Castro. "Perhaps that might have

---

[54] Del Valle, *Peligros y principios*, 91-2. Tripartite conference held in Antigua January 3-7, 1991.
[55] Del Valle, *Peligros y principios*, 97-8.

been the solution, if they had been simply for Cuba's defense rather than for strategic purposes."[56]

The measure of Cuba's military potential in October 1962 is given by the Soviet and Cuban troops, combined with the Cuban people's and Soviet troops' determination to struggle and their great combat morale.

At 3:50 p.m. on October 22, an hour and a half before the White House announced to the world that missiles had been discovered, Commander in Chief Fidel Castro ordered the Revolutionary Armed Forces placed on "combat alert"; at 5:35 p.m., he decreed a "combat alarm." Fifty-six infantry divisions were deployed in their positions; of them, 5 were permanent, 9 were cut-down and 40 were of the kind mobilized in time of war. There were also four brigades (one of tanks and three of artillery), 10 anti-landing battalions, six battalions of defensive artillery, three independent 120-mm. mortar groups, 20 naval units, 118 antiaircraft batteries and 47 combat aircraft. In all, 270,000 combatants were mobilized, 170,000 of whom were reservists, and 100,000, in active service in the Armed Forces. The members of the militia and People's Defense units brought the total to 400,000 armed combatants.[57]

On October 12, command of the U-2s that were flying over Cuba was transferred from the Central Intelligence Agency to the Joint Chiefs of Staff and the Strategic Air Command. On October 13, the planes were moved from Edwards Air Force Base, in California, to McCoy Air Force Base in Orlando, Florida — much closer to Cuba. It was from that base that the U-2 took off and flew over the island on the morning of October 14 and photographed the nuclear installations — photos that were developed and examined the next day. Kennedy was informed of the finding on the morning of October 16. In the following days, photos of other parts of Cuban territory were taken, and they showed excavations for missile launch pads and for fuel tanks, and conduits for cables leading from the center of each launch pad to a control bunker and other things that indicated the presence of ballistic missiles.[58]

Kennedy formed a high-level advisory group called ExComm, the Executive Committee of the U.S. National Security Council. Its statutory members included Vice-President Lyndon Johnson; Secretary of State Dean Rusk; Secretary of Defense Robert McNamara; Joint Chiefs of Staff Chairman General Maxwell Taylor; Special Assistant to

---

[56] Fidel Castro, Tripartite Conference.
[57] Del Valle, *Peligros y principios*, 141-2.
[58] Brugioni, *Eyeball to Eyeball*, 181 and 276.

the President for National Security Affairs McGeorge Bundy; CIA director John McCone; Secretary of the Treasury Douglas Dillon; Attorney General Robert Kennedy; Under Secretary of State George Ball; Deputy Secretary of Defense Roswell Gilpatric; and Ambassador-at-Large Llewellyn Thompson. In addition, the ExComm unofficially included U. Alexis Johnson, Deputy Under Secretary of State for Political Affairs; Assistant Secretary of Defense for International Security Paul Nitze; former Secretary of State Dean Acheson; private advisers John McCloy and Robert Lovett; U.S. Ambassador to the UN Adlai Stevenson; Deputy Director of the USIA Donald Wilson; Assistant Secretary of State for Inter-American Affairs Edwin Martin; and on the first day of the crisis, former U.S. Ambassador to the Soviet Union Charles Bohlen. Other specialists took part in the discussions as needed.[59] ExComm played a key role in the decisions Kennedy made during the crisis.

According to the documents that have been published and the revelations made by participants in the meetings of ExComm, all kinds of measures were considered for forcing the Soviets to withdraw the missiles from Cuba — all kinds of measures except negotiating with the Cuban government. Those options included a surprise air attack on Cuban targets, military invasion, a naval blockade and agreeing to withdraw the Jupiter missiles from Turkey if the Soviet missiles were withdrawn from Cuba. In October 1959, Eisenhower had signed an agreement with Turkey to install 15 nuclear missiles there, and Kennedy had authorized their installation in 1961; they were operational by March or April 1962, and no orders were given to dismantle them until the end of the crisis. In the summer of 1959, Khrushchev had complained to Vice-President Nixon about U.S. plans to send more missiles to Europe, including those in Turkey. During that meeting, Anastas Mikoyan had said that the missiles in Turkey were there to impose "political domination." Later, in Memorandum 181 of August 23, 1962, Kennedy asked that a study be made of what to do with the Jupiters in Turkey if the Soviet Union installed that kind of weapon in Cuba, warning that those in Turkey were defensive, while the weapons in Cuba would be offensive.[60]

On October 27, Khrushchev offered to make a deal concerning the missiles in Cuba and Turkey. In the 1992 Havana meeting, Raymond

---

[59] Chang and Kornbluh, *The Cuban Missile Crisis, 1962*, XXV, XXVI.
[60] Nathan, *The Cuban Missile Crisis Revisited*, essay by Barton J. Bernstein, "Reconsidering the Missile Crisis: Dealing with the problem of the American Jupiters in Turkey," 58-9.

Garthoff, a CIA analyst, said that the U.S. decision to withdraw the Jupiter missiles from Turkey and Italy was not the result of negotiations or later agreements. Robert Kennedy had taken up this topic in a talk with the Soviet ambassador in Washington on October 24 or 25 and again in the verbal understanding on October 27, because as Garthoff reported him saying, the United States was considering withdrawing the missiles from both countries. When asked how long it would be before this was done, he answered that he didn't know, but he thought it would be around four or five months.

The Jupiter missiles close to the borders of the Soviet Union had always worried the Soviet government. Khrushchev not only complained about them to Nixon in 1959 but had commented about them when he was in the Crimea with his Minister of Defense and it occurred to him to suggest to the Cuban leaders that nuclear missiles be installed on the island. He pointed out that the United States hadn't asked the Soviet Union's permission when it placed its missiles in Turkey, so the Soviet Union could do the same with Cuba.

The agreement with the Turkish government was also a cause of concern to Kennedy, for he thought the Soviets might react by placing nuclear missiles in Cuba to restore the strategic balance — as shown in his August 1962 memorandum, written when he didn't know that the members of the Soviet missile troop division were already on their way to Cuba. Later, in the midst of the crisis, he was on the point of publicly accepting the deal, according to revelations McGeorge Bundy made in 1987 during the conference the United States held on Hawk's Cay to analyze the events of 1962. Bundy said that on October 27 the President ordered Dean Rusk to talk with Andrew Cordier, then President of Columbia University and for many years a high-ranking official in the United Nations, to get him to give Secretary General U Thant the text of a statement proposing the missile withdrawal deal as if it were his own idea. The statement was to be given to the UN Secretary-General when Kennedy decided to go ahead with the plan, but this was never done.

Kennedy's discussions with the members of his group of advisers took place at the same time as a gigantic military mobilization. Declassified documents and statements by the members of ExComm have since made the details public. Troops were moved in the southeastern part of the United States, and several divisions — over 100,000 infantrymen and armored units — were regrouped in Florida and Texas. After October 22, the B-47 bombers of the Strategic Air Command — each carrying nuclear weapons — were dispersed in 40 civilian airports. The First Armored Division, which was en route to

Fort Stewart, and five other Army divisions were placed in a state of alert. To impose a naval blockade of Cuba, the Navy used 238 vessels: 8 aircraft carriers, 2 cruisers, 118 destroyers, 13 submarines, 65 amphibious craft and 32 auxiliary craft. A force of a quarter of a million men was available for the invasion of Cuba, as were enough planes to carry out 2,000 missions over its territory. In addition, there were 100 merchant vessels for carrying troops, and the Guantánamo Naval Base — in Cuban territory, but occupied by the United States — was reinforced with three Marine battalions, increasing its strength from 8,000 to 16,000 soldiers.

For its part, the government of the Soviet Union issued instructions on October 23 that the strategic missile troops, the members of the antiaircraft defense units and the fleet of submarines should retain those of their men who were to have been demobilized for reasons of age and that the programmed rest periods should be suspended. An order was sent to place all of the Soviet units in Cuba in a state of complete combat readiness, and the other Warsaw Pact countries took corresponding military measures.

The course of action taken by the Kennedy administration, imposing a naval blockade, was much discussed in ExComm, because its members had some doubts about its legality. It was an overt act of war which violated international law. Fidel Castro denounced it the same day it was imposed. "No country," he declared, "may stop the ships of another country on the high seas." He added, "Two violations are being committed: one against the sovereignty of Cuba and the other against the right of all the peoples," because the United States had declared that it would halt and search any ship from any country. That same day, Khrushchev said that it violated the international norms of freedom of navigation, and not only Cuba and the Soviet Union but also U.S. jurists and the Prime Minister of the United Kingdom supported that view. It was difficult for Washington to convince public opinion it was abiding by international law and the Charter of the United Nations. In his October 22 announcement of the discovery of the missiles, Kennedy stated that a strict "quarantine" would be imposed on "offensive" military materiel en route to Cuba; the next day, he decided to impose a blockade at 2:00 p.m. on October 24 based on a resolution that the Organization of American States had adopted that same day, October 23 — that is, after he had already decided to take that measure.

In ExComm's discussions, the word "quarantine" was used instead of "embargo," because "embargo" defined an act of war, whereas "quarantine" disguised it, making it easier for world public opinion to accept. During the Hawk's Cay talks in March 1987 and the Cambridge talks that same year between members of the Kennedy administration and academics, Abram Chayes, legal counsel at the State Department, said that Kennedy had refused to sign the proclamation ordering the naval blockade until the OAS reached an agreement — so he would have something on which to base his decision. Specialists on juridical questions objected to the measure. Professor Quincy Wright of Columbia University, honorary Vice-President of the American Society of International Law, said in a seminar that the Society held in April 1963 that it had been unfortunate that the United States had established the "quarantine," because, by so doing, it had resorted to a unilateral act of force that couldn't be reconciled with its obligations under the Charter of the United Nations, which required that disputes be solved by peaceful means and that neither force nor the threat of force be used in international relations. Professor Wright added: "The quarantine... deprived the Soviet Union of its right to 'freedom of the seas'... and [was] against the purposes of the United Nations to maintain international peace and bring about a peaceful settlement of international disputes (Article 2, paragraph 4)... and to submit all disputes not settled to the Security Council or other United Nations organs (Articles 35, 37). The issue was, it is true, submitted to the United Nations, but not until unilateral action had been proclaimed."[61]

Dean Acheson, one of the architects of the Cold War who was a champion in ExComm of the severest military measures against Cuba, raised a dissenting voice in that seminar. He didn't consider it important that the United States was entering a legal gray area, and he supported the naval blockade, just as he had done in the meetings in the White House.[62]

In London, in the messages he exchanged with Kennedy and with his ambassador to the United States, Prime Minister Harold McMillan, a U.S. ally closely identified with Washington's policy, also expressed doubts about the blockade's legality. In a message to the President, he said, "Of course the international lawyers will take the point that a blockade which involves the searching of ships of all countries is difficult to defend in peace time. Indeed quite a lot of controversy has gone on in the past about its use in war time."[63] He went on to say,

[61] Quincy Wright, Essay on Proceedings of the American Society of International Law, 57th meeting (Washington D.C.: Society, 1963), 9-10.
[62] Wright, Essay, 13, 14, 15.
[63] Harold Macmillan, *At the End of the Day* (London: Macmillan, 1973), 188.

"However, we must rest not so much on precedent as on the unprecedented condition of the modern world in a nuclear age."[64] But, in another message, a few days later, he stated, "Our traditional attitude with regard to the freedom of the seas would put us in an awkward position."[65]

In the Hawk's Cay conference, General Maxwell Taylor speculated on whether the Soviet Union would have sent its ships up to the line of the blockade "and stand there and scream to the world over the violation of international law we were indulging in, and meanwhile start that argument going while his missiles completed their readiness in the island."[66]

It is irrefutable that the U.S. government acted in a premeditated manner right from the first, using coercion while turning a blind eye to its international obligations, openly ignoring the sovereign right of Cuba — a country subjected to a dirty war and threatened with the military clout of a superpower only 90 miles away — forced to defend itself. It is clear that Cuba tried to improve its military capability, not for offensive purposes but to safeguard its territorial integrity.

Some U.S. historians have stated that Kennedy had to run the risk of war to obtain domestic political dividends, and they have denounced the naval blockade as an irresponsible action, saying that the peaceful solution of the crisis was due to Soviet moderation and the United States' good luck. That is the opinion of I. F. Stone, Ronald Steel and Barton J. Bernstein. Stone noted a clear divergence between the national interests of his country and the political interests of Kennedy. Stone called for establishing secret contacts with Khrushchev in hopes of solving the conflict through diplomatic means, but Kennedy decided on confrontation because it would more likely force Khrushchev to withdraw the missiles before the November election. "There was no time for prolonged negotiation, summit conference or UN debates if the damage was to be undone before the election."[67]

Steel emphasized Kennedy's political vulnerability with regard to Cuba and his need that the nuclear ballistic missiles be withdrawn before the election. Professor Bernstein of Stanford University said that Kennedy and his closest advisers felt impelled to do something that would impress Khrushchev and other Soviet leaders with U.S. decisiveness. "A public confrontation and a public triumph would

---

[64] Macmillan, *At the End of the Day*, 188.
[65] Ibid., 193.
[66] Blight and Welch, *On the Brink*, 79.
[67] Nathan, *The Cuban Missile Crisis Revisited*, 164.

allow him dramatically... [to] persuade various 'constituencies' — citizens at home, allies abroad, and the Soviets — of his decisiveness and commitment."[68] According to Bernstein, the Cuban confrontation was the supreme expression of the "potentially fatal paradox behind American strategic policy: that the country might have to go to war to affirm the very credibility that is supposed to make war unnecessary."[69] He stated that negotiation should have been used rather than confrontation.

John Kenneth Galbraith, Kennedy's ambassador to India at the time of the crisis, stated very clearly that domestic policy was a very important factor in the decision to impose the blockade: "Once [the missiles] were there... the political needs of the Kennedy administration urge it take almost any risk to get them out."[70]

Here, we should remember Khrushchev's observation on the role played by the Congressional election in the United States and his insistence on not making the military agreement with Cuba public before November 6, the date of the election, so as not to hurt Kennedy — for his adversaries might accuse him of having allowed the Soviet Union to install the missiles in Cuba. Khrushchev referred to the election on several occasions, and it seems that he planned the deployment of the nuclear weapons and troops in August and September precisely so they would be operational in November, believing that when he told Kennedy of their presence after the election Kennedy would accept the fait accompli with resignation and search for a peaceful solution, resisting electoral pressures.

When Kennedy learned on October 16 that nuclear weapons were in Cuba, he evidently felt that the Soviets had deceived him, because they had assured him several times that they would never take such a step, since their ICBMs were sufficient for their defense. Unconfirmed rumors of the presence of strategic weapons in Cuba had circulated in the United States in September and October, and the Republicans kept harping on this subject in the press and in Congress; Kennedy had denied the rumors. Subsequently, the U.S. President used the argument of the secret introduction of the ballistic missiles to great effect, for he presented it as an aggressive act. During the crisis he based his actions on this claim as well as his description of the Soviet arms, declaring that they were of an offensive nature and, therefore, posed a threat to the security of the United States.

---

[68] Ibid.
[69] Ibid.
[70] Ibid., 165.

Commenting on the public and private assurances that the Soviet government gave Washington that it would not install nuclear missiles in Cuba, Fidel Castro has said that the secrecy of the operation placed the Soviet Union and Cuba at a political and practical disadvantage.

Cuba always expressed the opinion that it would be best to make the military agreement public, because it had a sovereign right to make that decision. Similarly, it never allowed itself to be drawn into an argument about the nature of the weapons — whether they were offensive or defensive. The Soviets made the mistake, however, playing into Kennedy's hands, and Kennedy exploited the issue very well. He distributed maps to all the mass media in the region — maps with concentric circles showing the ranges of the missiles and emphasizing that their radii of action enabled them to reach such places as Mexico City, Caracas and Lima, apart from cities in the United States. He also stressed this when he went on television on October 22. The medium-range missiles, he said, could hit targets in Washington, D.C., the Panama Canal, Cape Canaveral, the Central American countries, and the Caribbean, while the intermediate-range missiles could reach targets as far away as Canada's Hudson Bay.

Because of the importance of the matter, members of the U.S. government held many discussions on what kind of weapons they were. The topic came up in a memorandum drafted by Norbert Schlei, assistant to the Attorney General, in response to a question about what to do if the Soviets installed strategic missiles in Cuba. Schlei said that it wasn't possible to do anything "if the missiles are defensive in nature. That's why the President chose to speak of 'offensive' missiles in his September 4 statement."[71] In that statement, the U.S. President said that an increase in the number of Soviet military personnel in Cuba had been detected but that there wasn't any evidence of an organized combat force, Russian bases, violations of the 1934 Pact on Guantánamo or the presence of ground-to-ground missiles or any other significant offensive capacity.

Abram Chayes, director of the Legal Department of the Department of State, has confirmed that it was the first time anyone had spoken of offensive weapons. He commented that in the meetings of ExComm, the legal grounds that were used to object to the missiles if they were described as offensive, was that their presence could be interpreted as an armed attack under Article 51 of the Charter of the United Nations — an argument which, Chayes said, the lawyers did not support.

---

[71] Blight and Welch, *On the Brink,* 79.

Article 51 states, "Nothing in the present Charter shall impair the inherent right of individual or collective self-defense if an armed attack occurs against a Member of the United Nations, until the Security Council has taken measures necessary to maintain international peace and security." How the U.S. hawks twisted and adulterated the juridical concepts and provisions of that international document to serve their aggressive purposes!

Chayes recalled that an "extremist" bill had been presented in the U.S. Congress calling for military action against Cuba, but the administration had managed to water it down. In its final form it warned of "dire consequences if offensive missiles were introduced into Cuba"[72] and made a distinction between offensive and defensive weapons, warning that the United States was better prepared to use military force in defense of its security if need be. "This resolution was used, by the way, as a justification for President Kennedy's quarantine proclamation,"[73] and the term "offensive weapons" was included in the resolution of the Organization of American States.

At the 1989 Hawk's Bay conference, Sorensen referred to the speculation about what actions the Soviets would take. He said that the line between offensive and defensive weapons was drawn in September "and it was not drawn in a way which was intended to leave the Soviets any ambiguity to play with."[74] He added that the President had drawn the line at a point he thought the Soviets wouldn't reach. Sorensen also said that, "legally, the Soviets had a perfect right to do what they did, so long as the Cuban government agreed. Kennedy clearly worried that the Soviets might be able to court world opinion by appealing to the canons of international law. So he urged [Sorensen, as a practitioner of international law] to put the 'emphasis on the sudden and deceptive' deployment."[75]

On the evening of October 22, Kennedy went on television from the White House, announcing that the Soviet Union had sent nuclear missiles to Cuba and that the United States would impose a naval blockade around Cuba.[76] That same day, the Cuban government drafted a letter to the President of the UN Security Council requesting an emergency meeting of that body "in view of the act of war unilaterally carried out by the government of the United States by giving instructions for a naval blockade of Cuba." The blockade, it said,

---

[72] Ibid., 40.
[73] Ibid., 41.
[74] Ibid., 43.
[75] Ibid., 391-n. 70.
[76] Hilsman, *To Move a Nation*, 210.

was being imposed behind the backs of the international agencies and "with absolute contempt" for the Security Council and created an immediate threat of war. On the same date, the government of the United States also requested "an emergency meeting of the Security Council be convoked without delay to take action against this latest Soviet threat to world peace."[77]

The UN's major discussion on the state of war between China and India was set aside to focus on the situation in the Caribbean. One day after the requests of Cuba and the United States, the Soviet Union called for a meeting of the Security Council to examine the U.S. violation of the Charter of the United Nations and threats to peace. On October 23, the Security Council decided to examine the letters from the three countries at the same time and to invite Cuba's representative to take part in the debate (Cuba wasn't a member of the Security Council).

Adlai Stevenson was the first to take the floor. He stated that when Cuba became a base for "offensive weapons" and weapons of mass destruction, it had created a threat to peace in the western hemisphere and the world, and that such a threat had forced the United States to impose the "quarantine" on all shipments of "offensive" military arms to Cuba. He said that the Soviet bases in Cuba were entirely different from the NATO bases near the Soviet Union, since the latter were of a defensive nature, compatible with the principles of the United Nations, whereas the Soviet bases in Cuba, which had been installed clandestinely, had created the most important nuclear base in the hemisphere outside of all existing treaties. He emphasized that the Security Council was faced with a serious matter and that the future of civilization might hang on its decision.

Immediately after this, Mario García Incháustegui, Cuba's representative, stated that his country had had to arm itself defensively because of repeated attacks by the United States. He recalled that Cuban President Osvaldo Dorticós had declared in the General Assembly that if the United States would give Cuba effective guarantees that it wouldn't engage in attacks on his country, Cuba would not need to strengthen its defenses. He pointed out that the United States, which had accused Cuba of being a threat, had committed countless acts of aggression against Cuba. The U.S. government had reserved for itself the right to determine when a missile was good and when a missile was bad, when a base was good and when a base was bad, and was pushing the world to the brink of

---

[77] Ibid., 211.

war. Cuba had always been willing to engage in negotiations to solve its conflicts with the United States, but its offers had always met with angry replies. He added that the naval blockade was a war measure and asked that the aggressive forces around Cuba's coasts be withdrawn.

Valerian Zorin, the representative of the Soviet Union, who was presiding over the Security Council at the time, observed that the Council had met in circumstances that were cause for very serious concern for peace in the Caribbean and in the entire world. The naval blockade of Cuba and the other military measures that the U.S. government had taken constituted a flagrant violation of the UN Charter and the principles of international law and a step toward thermonuclear war. He said that the Soviet government advocated the withdrawal of all foreign armaments and forces from foreign territories and would not be opposed to its being done under UN supervision.

On October 24, representatives of allies of the United States, Soviet allies and nonaligned countries spoke. Venezuela's representative expressed his concern over the threat to its security posed by the installation of nuclear missiles and bases in Cuba and said that the Security Council should take measures to keep nuclear weapons from reaching Cuba and ensure that the bases were dismantled. The representative of the United Kingdom stated that the introduction of Soviet nuclear missiles in the western hemisphere constituted a situation which those responsible for the security of the hemisphere could not tolerate. His country had never denied the Cuban people's right to choose their own political regime and to take whatever measures might be necessary to protect their government; likewise, his government had never denied the Cuban people's right to request military aid from another government. But, in view of the nature of the weapons and the secrecy which surrounded their introduction in Cuba, his government felt obliged to conclude that those bases were not exclusively defensive and that the Soviet government was trying to obtain an advantageous military position in Cuba.

The representative of Romania said that the military preparations for a new invasion of Cuba had begun before the discovery of certain offensive installations in Cuba and that the military blockade was an act of war that violated many international maritime declarations and agreements, such as the three agreements on the definition of aggression that had been signed in July 1933 — ratified by the United States. He asked the Security Council to denounce the United States for its action and to insist that the blockade be lifted and all intervention in the internal affairs of Cuba cease.

The representative of Ireland said that, while he understood the Cuban government's concern for its national security, the military strengthening in Cuba carried out with the help of the Soviet Union went beyond the need to buttress Cuba's defense capability. The representative of France immediately took the floor and stated that the introduction of offensive weapons in Cuba constituted a serious attempt to create a new war front in a region that had previously been free of nuclear weapons. The representative of China (Taiwan) then said that the United States was perfectly entitled to halt the continued flow of offensive weapons to Cuba when it saw its own security and that of its neighbors threatened. Then the Chilean representative said that the problem presented to the Security Council wasn't that of the Cuban revolution or of the infiltration of its communist ideology in other Latin American countries, but the fact that a power from another continent had found in Cuba a means for intervening in the western hemisphere and threatening its security.

In his contribution to the debate, the representative of the United Arab Republic reflected the feelings of the nonaligned countries. He said that the United States' unilateral decision to impose a quarantine in the Caribbean could not be condoned, for that measure not only was contrary to international law and the accepted norms of freedom of navigation on the high seas but also led to a situation that involved the risk of exacerbating world tension and of compromising international peace and security. He said that it was a measure adopted outside the United Nations, without the authorization of the Security Council, to which the founding members of the organization had entrusted the fundamental responsibility of maintaining international peace and security.

Both the Soviet Union and the United States presented draft resolutions to the Security Council, while Ghana and the United Arab Republic submitted another. The text of the Soviet document denounced the U.S. government's acts which violated the UN Charter and increased the threat of war. It maintained that Washington should revoke its decision to inspect the ships of other nations that were going to Cuba; asked that the United States cease and desist from its intervention in the internal affairs of Cuba; and urged that the United States, the Soviet Union and Cuba establish contacts and hold negotiations to normalize the situation and thus end the threat of war.

The U.S. draft requested that the missiles and "other offensive weapons" be dismantled and withdrawn from Cuba and authorized the Secretary-General to send a group of UN observers to Cuba to verify that the resolution was implemented. The document also stated that the "quarantine" imposed on military cargos to Cuba would be lifted after the withdrawal of the missiles had been verified, and recommended that the United States and the Soviet Union hold talks on the existing situation.

Right from the first, Washington excluded Cuba from all negotiations, it spoke of talks only between U.S. and Soviet negotiators; in contrast, the Soviet document included the Cubans in the proposed negotiations.

The night before this Security Council session, a meeting of the representatives of around 50 countries was held at UN headquarters. They spent three hours trying to find solutions that would stave off war and resolved to meet with the Secretary-General to communicate their concern. The participants decided that Ghana and the United Arab Republic, both members of the Security Council, should present a draft resolution in consultation with the other nonaligned countries whose representatives had already met. That draft requested the Secretary-General to urgently make contact with the parties directly involved, so as to examine appropriate measures that should be taken to end the threat to world peace and normalize the situation in the Caribbean. It called on the interested parties to abstain in the meantime from any action that, directly or indirectly, might aggravate the situation. The Security Council approved the resolution, and then a motion presented by Ghana and the United Arab Republic was adopted putting off its sessions sine die. No other sessions were ever held to look into this matter.

4

The letters

I t all began at 6:00 p.m. on the afternoon of October 22, when Foy Kohler, U.S. ambassador to the Soviet Union, entered the Kremlin to deliver a letter from the President of the United States to the Premier. The letter was accompanied by the text of a statement Kennedy was going to make in Washington an hour later, in which he would announce the discovery of the missiles and the establishment of a naval blockade of Cuba. Between that day and the month of December, more than 20 public and confidential letters would be exchanged by the U.S., Soviet and Cuban leaders in a dialogue by correspondence that was unprecedented in a conflict of such magnitude, since traditional diplomatic channels were seldom used. At the end of the crisis, Khrushchev and Fidel Castro sent each other five confidential letters which expressed the divergence in the positions they had adopted, misunderstandings by the Soviets, and the bitterness the Cubans felt over Moscow having come to an agreement with Washington behind Havana's back.

Kennedy's first letter had a very cold salutation. It began with "Sir" — not "Esteemed Premier," as did later letters. In that letter, Kennedy said that what had most concerned him in the discussions on Berlin and other international questions was the possibility that the Soviet government wouldn't interpret the wishes and determination of the United States correctly in a given situation, since he hadn't supposed that, in the Nuclear Age, the Soviet government would take the world into a war which no country could win and whose only result would be catastrophe for the entire world, including the aggressor.

Kennedy recalled that in the meeting they had in Vienna, he had stated very clearly that the United States would not tolerate any action on its part that would alter the balance of power, but, even so, strategic missiles had been installed in Cuba. He said that the United States was determined to wipe out that threat to the security of the nations in the western hemisphere and that the "minimal response" of the naval blockade shouldn't be taken as grounds for a mistaken assessment on his part.

Khrushchev replied the next day, saying that the measures the United States had taken constituted a serious threat to the peace and security of nations; that they flagrantly violated the Charter of the United Nations and the norms of navigation on the high seas and took the path of aggressive actions, both against Cuba and against the Soviet Union; and that they constituted clear interference in the internal affairs of the Republic of Cuba, the Soviet Union and other countries. Neither the UN Charter nor international norms gave any country the right to institute inspections in international waters of ships heading toward Cuban coasts, and, naturally, he couldn't allow any country to establish controls over the armaments of Cuba for strengthening its defense capability.

He reiterated that the armaments in Cuba, no matter what their classification, were only for its defense, to repulse attacks by an aggressor. He added that he hoped Kennedy would act wisely and renounce the actions he had undertaken, which might have catastrophic consequences for world peace.

Kennedy replied that Khrushchev should recognize that the Soviet Union had initiated the chain of events when it secretly supplied Cuba with offensive weapons and that, since the problem was being discussed in the UN Security Council, he recommended that both be prudent and not do anything that might make it harder to control the situation.

On October 24, Khrushchev sent a letter to Kennedy asking how he would react having received an ultimatum such as the one Kennedy himself had formulated. He said:

I think you would have been indignant at such a step on our part. And this would have been understandable to us... By what right did you do this? Our ties with the Republic of Cuba, like our relations with other states, regardless of what kind of states they may be, concern only these two countries and their bilateral relations. And if we now speak of the quarantine to which your letter refers, a quarantine may be established, according to accepted international practice, only by agreement of states between themselves, and not by some third party... Quarantines exist for example, on agricultural goods and products. But in this case the question is in no way one of quarantine, but rather of far more serious things, and you yourself understand this.

You, Mr President, are not declaring a quarantine, but rather are setting forth an ultimatum and threatening that if we do not give in to your demands you will use force. Consider what you are saying! And you want to persuade me to agree to this! What would it mean to agree to these demands? It would mean guiding one's relations with other countries not by reason, but by submitting to arbitrariness... No, Mr President, I cannot agree to this, and I think that in your own heart you recognize that I am correct. I am convinced that in my place you would act the same way.[78]

Khrushchev went on to say:

Reference to the decision of the Organization of American States cannot in any way substantiate the demands now advanced by the United States. This Organization has absolutely no authority or basis for adopting decisions such as the one you speak of in your letter. Therefore, we do not recognize these decisions... And you are doing all this not only out of hatred for the Cuban people and its government but also because of considerations of the election campaign in the United States. What morality, what law can justify such an approach by the American government to international affairs? No such morality or law can be found, because the actions of the United States with regard to Cuba constitute outright banditry or, if you like, the folly of degenerate imperialism. Unfortunately, such folly can bring grave suffering to the peoples of all countries, and to no lesser degree to the American people themselves, since the United States has completely lost its former isolation with the advent of modern types or armament... The Soviet government considers that the violation of the freedom to use international waters and international airspace is an act of aggression which pushes mankind toward the abyss of a nuclear-missile war. Therefore, the

---

[78] Chang and Kornbluh, *The Cuban Missile Crisis, 1962*, 163.

Soviet government cannot instruct the captains of Soviet vessels bound for Cuba to observe the orders of American naval forces blockading that island. Our instructions to Soviet mariners are to observe strictly the universally accepted norms of navigation in international waters and not to retreat one step from them. And if the American side violates these rules, it must realize what responsibility will rest upon it. Naturally we will not simply be bystanders to acts of piracy by American ships on the high seas. We will then be forced on our part to take the measures we consider necessary and adequate in order to protect our rights. We have everything necessary to do so.[79]

On October 25, Kennedy wrote that he was very sorry Khrushchev seemed not to have understood why he had taken that course of action.

In August there were reports of important shipments of military equipment and technicians from the Soviet Union to Cuba. In early September I indicated very plainly that the United States would regard any shipment of offensive weapons as presenting the gravest issues. After that time, this government received the most explicit assurances from your government and its representatives, both publicly and privately, that no offensive weapons were being sent to Cuba... In reliance on those solemn assurances I urged restraint upon those in this country who were urging action in this matter at that time. And then I learned beyond doubt what you have not denied — namely, that all these public assurances were false and that your military people had set out recently to establish a set of missile bases in Cuba... In the light of this record these activities in Cuba required the responses I have announced.[80]

On October 26, everything indicated a fateful outcome of the situation. Fidel Castro sent Khrushchev a letter warning him of this. (Because of its importance and the twisted interpretation that it was given in Moscow, I will quote it extensively later on and include Khrushchev's reply.) That same day, the Soviet Premier replied to Kennedy's letter of October 25 and proposed that, if he promised not to invade Cuba, the Soviet military specialists' presence in Cuba "would disappear." Some

---

[79] Ibid., 164.
[80] Ibid., 173.

of the main paragraphs in Khrushchev's letter which radically changed the situation appear below:

I assure you on behalf of the Soviet government and the Soviet people that your arguments regarding offensive weapons in Cuba are utterly unfounded. From what you have written me it is obvious that our interpretations on this point are different, or rather that we have different definitions for one type of military means or another. And indeed, the same types of armaments may in actuality have different interpretations…

You are mistaken if you think that any of our armaments in Cuba are offensive. However, let us not argue at this point. Evidently, I shall not be able to convince you. But I tell you, Mr President, you are a military man and you must understand: How can you possibly launch an offensive even if you have an enormous number of missiles of various ranges and power on your territory, using these weapons alone? These missiles are a means of annihilation and destruction. But it is impossible to launch an offensive by means of these missiles, even nuclear missiles of 100 megaton yield, because it is only people — troops — who can advance. Without people any weapons, whatever their power, cannot be offensive.

How can you, therefore, give this completely wrong interpretation, which you are now giving, that some weapons in Cuba are offensive, as you say? All weapons there — and I assure you of this — are of a defensive nature; they are in Cuba solely for the purpose of defense, and we have sent them to Cuba at the request of the Cuban government. And you say that they are offensive weapons.

But, Mr President, do you really seriously think that Cuba could launch an offensive upon the United States and that even we, together with Cuba, could advance against you from Cuban territory? Do you really think so? How can that be? We do not understand…

You have now declared acts of piracy, the kind that were practiced in the Middle Ages when ships passing through international waters were attacked, and you have called this a "quarantine" around Cuba. Our vessels will probably soon enter the zone patrolled by your Navy. I assure you that the vessels which are now headed for Cuba are carrying the most innocuous peaceful cargos. Do you really think that all we do is to transport so-called offensive weapons, atomic and hydrogen bombs?…

Therefore, Mr President, let us show good sense. I assure you that the ships bound for Cuba are carrying no armaments at all. The armaments needed for the defense of Cuba are already there. I do not mean to say that there have been no shipments of armaments at all. No, there were such shipments. But now Cuba has already obtained the necessary weapons for defense.

Let us normalize relations. We have received an appeal from U Thant, Acting Secretary-General of the UN, containing his proposals. His proposals are to the effect that our side not ship any armaments to Cuba for a certain period of time while negotiations are being conducted — and we are prepared to enter into such negotiations — and the other side not undertake any acts of piracy against vessels navigating on the high seas. I consider these proposals reasonable. This would be a way out of the situation which has evolved that would give nations a chance to breathe easily...

We were very grieved by the fact — I spoke of this in Vienna — that a landing occurred and an attack made on Cuba [at the Bay of Pigs], as a result of which many Cubans were killed. You yourself told me then that this had been a mistake. I regarded that explanation with respect. You repeated it to me several times, hinting that not everyone occupying a high position would acknowledge his mistakes as you did. I appreciate such frankness... We have also acknowledged the mistakes which have been made in the history of our state, and have not only acknowledged them but have sharply condemned them.

You once said that the United States is not preparing an invasion. But you have also declared that you sympathize with the Cuban counterrevolutionary emigrants, support them, and will help them in carrying out their plans against the present government of Cuba. Nor is it any secret to anyone that the constant threat of armed attack and aggression has hung and continues to hang over Cuba. It is only this that has prompted us to respond to the request of the Cuban government to extend it our aid in strengthening the defense capability of that country.

If the President and government of the United States would give their assurances that the United States would itself not take part in an attack upon Cuba and would restrain others from such action; if you recall your Navy — this would immediately change everything. I do not speak for Fidel Castro, but I think that he and the government of Cuba would, probably, announce a demobilization. Then the question of armaments would also be

obviated, because when there is no threat, armaments are only a
burden for any people. This would also change the approach to
the question of destroying not only the armaments which you call
offensive, but of every other kind of armament...

Let us therefore display statesmanlike wisdom. I propose: we,
for our part, will declare that our ships bound for Cuba are not
carrying any armaments. You will declare that the United States
will not invade Cuba with its troops and will not support any
other forces which might intend to invade Cuba. Then the
necessity for the presence of our military specialists in Cuba will
be obviated...[81]

October 26 and 27 were days filled with uncertainty and confusion
from first to last. The first installment of this last letter from the Soviet
leader reached the State Department in Washington at 6:00 p.m., via
the U.S. embassy in Moscow. It was sent in four parts, the last of which
arrived at 9:00 p.m., 12 hours after the text had been delivered to the
U.S. embassy in the Soviet capital. At 10:00 p.m., Kennedy called his
advisers together to analyze Khrushchev's message and his possible
reply.

At 1:30 on the afternoon of that same day, Friday, October 26,
Alexander Fomin, an official at the Soviet embassy, called John Scali, of
ABC television, and asked him to meet him. He asked Scali if his
friends in the State Department, where he was accredited as a
journalist, would be interested in solving the crisis along the following
lines: (1) the Soviet Union would agree to dismantle the launching pads
and withdraw the missiles; (2) it would allow the United Nations to
supervise and inspect the withdrawal of the missiles; (3) the Soviet
Union would pledge never again to introduce missiles into Cuba; and
(4) the United States would publicly pledge not to invade Cuba.
According to this account, the meeting between the journalist and the
diplomat took place hours before Khrushchev's letter arrived, and its
message was similar to that of the Premier's letter. It should be pointed
out that both participants have confirmed the time of their meeting.

Scali went back to the State Department and told Roger Hilsman,
Director of the Bureau of Intelligence and Research, about the meeting,
and Hilsman told Dean Rusk. Rusk said that Scali should see Fomin
again and tell him that the government was interested in the

---

[81] Ibid., 186-8.

suggestion, but the matter would have to be taken care of in one or two days.[82]

At 7:00 a.m. on October 26, the first foreign ship was searched by a U.S. Naval ship. Men from the destroyer *Joseph P. Kennedy, Jr.* boarded the freighter *Marucla*, owned by a Panamanian company but flying the Libyan flag. On seeing that the cargo wasn't of interest, they allowed it to go on to Cuba.

In Cuba, Fidel Castro visited the Soviet embassy late at night on October 26 and stayed through the early hours of October 27 drafting a letter to Khrushchev. This followed a meeting with the Soviet military command where he informed them that he had given orders to shoot at the U.S. planes that were flying close to the ground, because of the threat they posed. (In the 1992 meeting held in Havana to analyze the crisis, Fidel Castro explained that, on that night of October 26, faced with the threat of an attack on Cuba, he hadn't seen any way out of the situation.) The letter was to encourage Khrushchev and strengthen his moral position. Fidel Castro knew that the Soviet leader was suffering greatly. He was also afraid that mistakes might be made, that there would be a lack of decisiveness, something he had already noted. That was why Fidel Castro decided to give Khrushchev some ideas about what he thought should be done if an invasion took place and an attempt made to occupy the country. He was convinced that an invasion would turn into a thermonuclear war, which is why he made the recommendation that was misinterpreted in Moscow. Fidel Castro was aware of the mistake the Soviets had made at the time of the Nazi attack in World War II, which had caught them unawares.

The letter was sent from Havana early on the morning of October 27; the formula for the solution to the crisis had already been outlined in Moscow. Fidel Castro didn't know this, just as he was unaware that Khrushchev had sent a letter to Kennedy on October 26 in which he considered the possibility of withdrawing the missiles. Meanwhile, work on the launching pads and other installations continued. In Washington, the President was directing the State Department to proceed in organizing a civilian government for Cuba, to be established after the occupation of the country. On the evening of October 26, Robert Kennedy met with the Soviet ambassador in Washington and told him that the U.S. missiles that were in Turkey might be considered in a deal.

The following is the letter Fidel Castro sent to Khrushchev on October 26:

---

[82] Hilsman, *To Move a Nation*, 217-8.

From an analysis of the situation and the reports in our possession, I consider that the aggression is almost imminent within the next 24 to 72 hours.

There are two possible variants: the first and most likely is an air attack against certain targets with the limited objective of destroying them; the second, less probable although possible, is invasion. I understand that this variant would call for a large number of forces and it is, in addition, the most repulsive form of aggression, which might inhibit them.

You can rest assured that we will firmly and resolutely resist attack, whatever it may be.

The morale of the Cuban people is extremely high and the aggressor will be confronted heroically.

At this time I want to convey to you briefly my personal opinion.

If the second variant is implemented and the imperialists invade Cuba with the goal of occupying it, the danger that such aggressive policy poses for humanity is so great that following such an event, the Soviet Union must never allow the circumstances in which the imperialists could launch the first nuclear strike against it.

I tell you this because I believe that the imperialists' aggressiveness is extremely dangerous and if they actually carry out the brutal act of invading Cuba in violation of international law and morality, that would be the moment to eliminate such danger forever through an act of clear legitimate defense, however harsh and terrible the solution would be, for there is no other.

My opinion has been influenced by seeing how this aggressive policy is developing, how the imperialists, disregarding world public opinion and ignoring principles and law, are blockading the seas, violating our airspace and preparing an invasion, while at the same time frustrating every possibility for talks, even though they are aware of the seriousness of the problem.

You have been and continue to be a tireless defender of peace and I realize how bitter these hours must be, when the outcome of your superhuman efforts is so seriously threatened. However, up to the last moment we will maintain the hope that peace will be safeguarded and we are willing to contribute to this as much as we can. But at the same time, we are ready to calmly confront a situation which we view as quite real and quite close.

Once more I convey to you the infinite gratitude and recognition of our people to the Soviet people who have been so generous and fraternal with us, as well our profound gratitude and admiration for you, and wish you success in the huge task and serious responsibilities ahead of you.[83]

Ambassador Alexeev has provided details about the circumstances in which Fidel Castro wrote this letter. He said that it was 2:00 a.m. on October 27. He and Soviet First Secretary Monakhov were there with Fidel Castro. The Prime Minister was dictating to Monakhov, who didn't know Spanish very well — which is why Fidel Castro thought he might have gotten something wrong when Khrushchev, thinking he had been advised to make a preemptive strike, reacted in an unexpected way. The letter was written in Russian; another functionary, Darusenko, translated Fidel Castro's notes. At the same time, Alexeev sent a short cable to Moscow reporting that a letter was being drafted and that an air strike was expected in 24 to 48 hours. The cable reached Moscow at 2:00 p.m. (a.m. on October 27, Eastern Standard Time) and the letter, at 1:00 a.m. on October 28 (p.m. of October 27, Eastern Standard Time).

The members of ExComm met again in the White House at 10:00 a.m. on October 27 to continue analyzing Khrushchev's letter of the day before. While they were doing so, at 11:03 a.m. a second message came in from the Soviet leader. In part, it said:

You wish to ensure the security of your country, and this is understandable. But Cuba, too, wants the same thing; all countries want to maintain their security. But how are we, the Soviet Union, our government, to assess your actions which are expressed in the fact that you have surrounded the Soviet Union with military bases; placed military bases literally around our country; and stationed your missile armaments there? This is no secret. Responsible Americans openly declare that it is so. Your missiles are located in Britain, are located in Italy, and are aimed at us. Your missiles are located in Turkey.

You are disturbed over Cuba. You say that this disturbs you because it is 90 miles by sea from the coast of the United States of America. But Turkey adjoins us; our sentries patrol back and forth and see each other. Do you consider, then, that you have the right to demand security for your own country and the removal of the

---

[83] Chang and Kornbluh, *The Cuban Missile Crisis, 1962*, 189.

weapons you call offensive, but do not accord the same right to us? You have placed destructive missile weapons, which you call offensive, in Turkey, literally next to us. How then can recognition of our equal military capacities be reconciled with such unequal relations between our great states? This is irreconcilable...

I therefore make this proposal: We are willing to remove from Cuba the [missiles] which you regard as offensive. We are willing to carry this out and to make this pledge in the United Nations. Your representatives will make a declaration to the effect that the United States, for its part, considering the uneasiness and anxiety of the Soviet government, will remove its comparable [missiles] from Turkey. Let us reach agreement as to the period of time needed by you and by us to bring this about. And, after that, persons entrusted by the United Nations Security Council could inspect on the spot the fulfillment of the pledges made. Of course, the permission of the governments of Cuba and Turkey is necessary for the entry into those countries of these representatives and for the inspection of the fulfillment of the pledge made by each side. It would be best if these representatives enjoyed the confidence of the Security Council, as well as both the United States and the Soviet Union, and also that of Turkey and Cuba. I do not think it would be difficult to select people who would enjoy the trust and respect of all parties concerned.[84]

The Kremlin's offer of a deal involving the nuclear weapons in Cuba and those in Turkey caused consternation in the White House. Countless replies were discussed, and Kennedy said he couldn't make any public commitment involving the missiles in Turkey and Italy, because to do so would create problems with his NATO allies. Another meeting of ExComm was called for 4:00 p.m. The pros and cons of military aggression were discussed at length. The President and his advisers considered that, in view of the first letter (the one dated October 26, which they hadn't yet answered), the offer of a missile deal showed that Khrushchev was upping his price for the withdrawal of the missiles from Cuba. In the midst of that discussion, some more alarming news reached the White House. It was confirmed that a U-2 plane had been shot down in eastern Cuba. The Soviet missile troops had shot at the spy plane. General Gribkov recalled later that Soviet Minister of Defense Malinowsky had telegraphed the Soviet command

---

[84] Ibid., 197-8.

in Cuba, "You have been precipitate in shooting the plane down while our negotiations with the U.S. authorities are progressing successfully."[85]

When Fidel Castro gave the order to fire on the planes that were flying close to the ground, the Soviet military chief, in turn, ordered the antiaircraft missile troops to be in full combat readiness, and the whole radiotechnical observation system (radars) was engaged. In the 1992 Havana meeting, it was reported that General Stepan Naumovich Grechko gave the order to shoot down the plane. The pilot of the plane was Major Rudolf R. Anderson, Jr., one of the first who had flown over Cuba at the beginning of the crisis.

The members of ExComm hadn't yet come to an agreement on how to reply to Khrushchev's last two letters. Several drafts were drawn up that weren't accepted, and the White House issued a statement saying that, "Several inconsistent and conflicting proposals have been made by the Soviet Union within the last 24 hours... an end to further work on the Cuban bases was said to be 'an urgent preliminary' to consideration of any proposal made by the Soviet Union."[86]

In the end, they decided to ignore the letter proposing the deal involving the Jupiter missiles in Turkey and to answer only the first message, which outlined the agreement to provide Cuba with guarantees that there would be no invasion and to withdraw the military personnel and missiles from the island. Kennedy's response to Khrushchev's letter that didn't mention Turkey was sent to Moscow at 8:05 p.m.; no reply was made to the second message, dated October 27.[87]

Among other things, the U.S. President said the following:

The first thing that needs to be done, however, is for work to cease on offensive missile bases in Cuba and for all weapons systems in Cuba capable of offensive use to be rendered inoperable, under effective United Nations arrangements.

Assuming this is done promptly, I have given my representatives in New York instructions that will permit them to work out this week — in cooperation with the Acting Secretary-General and your representative — an arrangement for a

---

[85] A.I. Gribkov, Tripartite Conference, second session, January 10, 1992, 18. Translated from Spanish.
[86] *The Cuban Missile Crisis, 1962: A Chronology*, 73.
[87] Ibid.

permanent solution to the Cuban problem along the lines suggested in your letter of October 26...

If you will give your representative similar instructions, there is no reason why we should not be able to complete these arrangements and announce them to the world within a couple of days. The effect of such a settlement on easing world tensions would enable us to work toward a more general arrangement regarding "other armaments," as proposed in your second letter which you made public. I would like to say again that the United States is very much interested in reducing tensions and halting the arms race; and if your letter signifies that you are prepared to discuss a détente affecting NATO and the Warsaw Pact, we are quite prepared to consider with our allies any useful proposals.

But the first ingredient, let me emphasize, is the cessation of work on missile sites in Cuba and measures to render such weapons inoperable, under effective international guarantees. The continuation of this threat, or a prolonging of this discussion concerning Cuba by linking these problems to the broader questions of European and world security, would surely lead to an intensification of the Cuban crisis and a grave risk to the peace of the world.[88]

Neither the Cuban government nor the Soviet military officers who were in Cuba knew of the messages Khrushchev had sent to Kennedy on October 26 and 27. Moscow was offering formulas — incoherent formulas — for solving the crisis, and the third country involved, the protagonist in the crisis, didn't know what was going on. Following logical reasoning, it was very difficult to suppose that the Soviet Union would surrender its positions in exchange for empty promises, especially without consulting Cuba. The rapid change of direction of Khrushchev's letters came as a surprise to both the Cubans and the U.S. authorities. It is imaginable that it was difficult for the White House to feel sure of its ground regarding the letters from Moscow, because they raised obstacles that Kennedy and his advisers hadn't foreseen. The tone of the first message, describing the U.S. reaction as a serious threat to peace, and of the second letter, stating that the blockade was an action of pirates and that the Soviet ships wouldn't accept it but would defend their right to navigate freely on the high seas — and the censure contained in other messages — were a far cry from the tone of the last

[88] Ibid., 223.

missives and the unexpected offer of a deal: the missiles in Cuba for those in Turkey.

Likewise, Khrushchev's first letters to Kennedy gave Havana the impression that the Soviet Union would staunchly defend the universally accepted principles which the United States had violated. They also indicated that the Soviet Union would stand by the daring initiative it had made by installing the atomic missiles and the immense effort it had made of sending Cuba a fighting force of tens of thousands of men and artillery to defend the positions they had taken up on the island. It was even less comprehensible that the official argument of strengthening Cuba's defense capability with nuclear weapons so it could dissuade the United States from carrying out an invasion would be thrown aside and the missiles used as pawns to be swapped for the U.S. missiles in Turkey and Italy. It was inconceivable that Cuba wouldn't even be informed of what was going on.

An objective analysis of the letters exchanged between Moscow and Washington leads to the conclusion that the Soviet Union hesitated — while the United States at all times maintained a position of force and of threats against Cuba and the Soviet Union. With regard to Cuba, the United States never stopped considering the option of military aggression, air strikes, the occupation of the country to install a government that would do Washington's bidding, and the elimination of the revolution. The very fact that it refused to let Cuba participate in any of the discussions and never took Cuba's interests into account, but rather strove to maintain its aggressive policy against Cuba, was in sharp contrast to Cuba's constant defense of the supreme interests of the Soviet people, as shown in Fidel Castro's October 26 letter to Khrushchev, and its constant denunciations of the United States' offensive aims. Moreover, Havana always strictly upheld its principles.

Kennedy and his advisers remained in permanent session from October 16 to 28; and he and a smaller group of advisers continued to meet until January 7, 1963, when the three countries sent their messages to the Security Council, ending the process of negotiations and eliminating the possibility of a broad debate in the United Nations — since, as I've already noted, the Security Council's last meeting on this subject was held on October 25. This, too, worked against Cuba, as it became impossible for its representatives to present Cuba's criteria in the United Nations, which was supposed to be mediating in the conflict. It also closed off the possibility of continuing the discussion about one of the main aspects of the crisis: the search for what was called the long-term solution, a formula that would end the United

States' aggressive policy toward Cuba, which lay at the root of the whole conflict.

In the White House, discussions centered on forcing the Soviets to withdraw the missiles and not allowing the Cuban revolution to go its own way. The U.S. administration was concerned about getting the missiles withdrawn, which it managed to achieve, but the Cuban people and government, during and after the crisis, refused to let the United States dictate to them.

At 9:00 a.m. on October 28, the following message from Khrushchev to Kennedy was made public over Radio Moscow:

I have received your message of October 27, 1962. I express my satisfaction and gratitude for the sense of proportion and understanding you have shown of the responsibility you presently bear for the preservation of peace throughout the world. I very well understand your anxiety and the anxiety of the people of the United States that the weapons which you describe as "offensive" are, in fact, grim weapons. Both you and I understand what kind of weapons they are.

We wish to give confidence to all people longing for peace, and to calm the American people, who, I am certain, want peace as much as the people of the Soviet Union. In order to complete with greater speed the resolution of the conflict — one so dangerous to the cause of peace — the Soviet government, in addition to previously issued instructions on the cessation of further work at building sites for the weapons, has issued a new order on the dismantling of the weapons which you describe as "offensive." This order also calls for their crating and return to the Soviet Union.

Mr President, I would like to repeat once more what I had already written to you in my preceding letters: The Soviet government has placed economic aid at the disposal of the Cuban government, as well as arms, inasmuch as Cuba and the Cuban people have constantly been under the danger of an invasion.

The shelling of Havana took place from a pirate ship. It is said that irresponsible emigres did the shooting. This is possibly the case. However, the question arises: From where did they fire? After all, these Cubans have no territory, they have no private means, and they have no means to wage military action. Somebody placed in their hands the arms needed to shell Havana and carry out their piracy in the Caribbean — in Cuban territorial waters!

It is unthinkable in our time not to notice a pirate ship, particularly if one takes into account the presence of U.S. ships in the Caribbean from which all this is watched and observed. In such circumstances, pirate ships are freely moving around Cuba, shelling Cuba, and carrying out piracy upon peaceful transport vessels! It is, after all, known that they even shelled a British freighter!

In short, Cuba has been under the constant threat of aggressive forces which did not conceal their intentions to invade Cuban territory.

The Cuban people want to build their own country without outside interference. They are right in this, and one cannot blame them because they want to be masters of their own country and dispose of the fruits of their labor. The threat of an invasion of Cuba and all the other plans aimed at bringing about tension in Cuba are designed to engender uncertainty among the Cuban people, intimidate them, and hinder them in building their new life undisturbed.

Mr President, I want to say clearly again that we could not be indifferent to this. The Soviet government decided to help Cuba with means of defense against aggression — and only with means for purposes of defense.

We stationed means of defense there which you call offensive. We stationed them there in order that no attack should be made against Cuba and that no rash action should be permitted to take place.

I respect and trust your statement in the message of October 27, 1962, that no attack will be made on Cuba — that no invasion will take place — not only by the United States, but also by other countries of the western hemisphere. The motives which prompted us to give aid of this nature to Cuba then cease. They are no longer applicable. Hence we have instructed our officers — and these [missiles], as I have already stated, are in the hands of Soviet officers — to take the necessary measures for stopping the building of the said projects, and their dismantling and return to the Soviet Union.

As I already told you in my letter of October 27, we both agree to come to an agreement that UN representatives could verify the dismantling of these [missiles].

In this way, if one is to rely on the assurances which you have made and on our orders to dismantle, then all necessary conditions appear to exist for resolving the conflict which has arisen.

I note with satisfaction that you have responded to my wish that the dangerous situation should be resolved and also that conditions should be created for a more thoughtful appraisal of the international situation which is fraught with great dangers in our age of thermonuclear weapons, rocket technology, space ships, global rockets and other lethal weapons. All people are interested in ensuring peace. Therefore, we who are invested with trust and great responsibility must not permit an exacerbation of the situation and must resolve a dangerous situation which has been fraught with serious consequences for the cause of peace. If we succeed, along with you and with the aid of other people of goodwill, in resolving this tense situation, we must also concern ourselves to see that other dangerous conflicts do not arise which might lead to a world thermonuclear catastrophe.

In conclusion, I wish to speak of the relations between NATO and the countries of the Warsaw Pact, which you mention. We have long ago spoken of this and are ready to continue an exchange of opinions with you on this question and find a reasonable solution. I also wish to continue an exchange of opinions on the prohibition of atomic and thermonuclear weapons, general disarmament and the lessening of international tension.

Mr President, I trust your statement. However, on the other hand, there are people in positions of power who would like to carry out an invasion of Cuba at this time, and in such a way to spark a war. If we take practical steps and announce the dismantling and evacuation of the relevant [missiles] from Cuba, then we wish to ensure at the same time that the Cuban people are confident that we are with them. We will not divest ourselves of the responsibility of granting help to them.

We are convinced that the people of all countries, like yourself, Mr President, will understand that we do not issue threats. We desire only peace. Our country is now on the upsurge. Our people are enjoying the fruits of their peaceful labor. They have achieved tremendous successes since the [1917] October Revolution and created supreme material and spiritual-cultural treasures. Our country is making use of those treasures and wants to develop its successes further and by its steadfast labor ensure further development on the road of peace and social progress.

I should like, Mr President, to remind you that military reconnaissance aircraft have violated the frontier of the Soviet Union, resulting in a conflict between our countries. An exchange of notes took place.

In 1960, we shot down your U-2 aircraft in the reconnaissance flight over the Soviet Union, which led to the wrecking of the [superpowers] meeting in Paris. You then took a correct position in condemning that criminal action by the former government of the United States. However, during the period of your tenure of office as president, a second violation of our frontier by an American U-2 aircraft took place in the Sakhalin area. We wrote to you about this violation on August 30. You replied that this violation had taken place as the result of bad weather and gave an assurance that it would not be repeated. We gave credence to your assurance because there was indeed bad weather in the area at that time. However, if your aircraft did not have the task of flying near our territory, then even bad weather could not cause an American aircraft to enter our airspace.

The conclusion follows that it was done with the knowledge of the Pentagon, which tramples on international practices and violates the frontiers of other states.

An even more dangerous case occurred on October 28 when your reconnaissance aircraft intruded into the northern territory of the Soviet Union, in the area of the Chukotka Peninsula, and flew over our territory.

One asks, Mr President, how should we regard this? What is it? A provocation? Your aircraft violate our frontier and in times as anxious as those which we are now experiencing, when everything has been placed in a state of combat readiness. An intruding American aircraft can easily be taken for a bomber with nuclear weapons, and this could push us toward a fatal step — all the more so because both the U.S. government and the Pentagon have long been saying that bombers with atomic bombs are constantly on duty in your country.

Therefore, you can imagine what kind of responsibility we assume, especially during the anxious times we are now living.

I would like to ask you to assess this correctly and take steps in order that it not serve as a provocation for unleashing war.

I would also like to express the following wish, which is perhaps more of a matter for the Cuban people. You do not at present maintain any diplomatic relations, but through my officers in Cuba I have reports that flights of American aircraft over Cuba are being carried out. We are interested that there should not be any war at all in the world, and the Cuban people should live in peace. However, Mr President, it is no secret that we have our people in Cuba. According to the treaty with the Cuban government, we have officers and instructors there who are training the Cubans. They are mainly ordinary people — experts, agronomists, technicians, irrigation and soil improvement experts, ordinary workers, tractor drivers and others. We are concerned about them.

I would like to ask you, Mr President, to bear in mind that a violation of Cuban airspace by American aircraft may also have dangerous consequences. If you do not want this, then no pretext should be given for the creation of a dangerous situation.

We must now be very cautious and not take such steps which will be of no use for the defense of the states involved in the conflict, but which are likely to arouse only irritation and even prove to be a provocation leading to the baneful step. We must, therefore, display sobriety and wisdom and refrain from steps of this sort.

We value peace, perhaps even more than other people, because we experienced the terrible war against Hitler. However, our people will not flinch in the face of any ordeal. Our people trust their government, and we assure our people and the world public that the Soviet government will not allow itself to be provoked.

Should the provocateurs unleash a war, they would not escape the grave consequences of such a war. However, we are confident that reason will triumph. War will not be unleashed and the peace and security of people will be assured!

In connection with negotiations in progress between UN Acting Secretary-General U Thant and representatives of the Soviet Union, the United States, and the Republic of Cuba, the Soviet government has sent Soviet First Deputy Minister of Foreign Affairs Kuznetsov to New York with a view to assisting U Thant in his noble efforts aimed at resolving the present dangerous situation.[89]

Khrushchev's letter arrived at 11:00 a.m. on Sunday, October 28. Kennedy and some advisers who had taken part in the meetings of ExComm since the beginning of the crisis felt relieved, as their

---

[89] Ibid., 226-9.

published accounts testify — but that wasn't the reaction of some of the military chiefs. Two of the most important military figures expressed their disgust over the solution that had been agreed to, because it left the Cuban revolution intact. Admiral George Anderson, Chief of Naval Operations, exclaimed loudly that the U.S. authorities "have been had"[90] and General Curtis LeMay, Chief of the Air Force, indignantly asked the members of the ExComm who were there at the time: "Why don't we go in and make a strike on Monday anyway?"[91] During the Vietnam War, LeMay recommended that the Vietnamese be bombed "back into the Stone Age." [92]

At 1:30 p.m., when the Soviet Premier's message was already known, four U.S. government officials left Washington and headed for New York, hoping to persuade U Thant to order an immediate inspection of the bases in Cuba, since the Soviets had agreed to this. The U.S. administration had quickly examined the technical details of the operation, saying that the job could be done from C-130 transport planes flying low with the doors open. They would be situated at Fort Stewart in Georgia and would be painted white, with the initials of the United Nations. At around 2:30 p.m., the four — Michael Forrestal, on the White House staff; Joseph Charyk, Under Secretary of the Air Force; and Abram Chayes and Joseph Siscoe, of the State Department — arrived at Stevenson's office in New York to tell him of their proposals. The ambassador told them that U Thant wouldn't act on his own authority and that he wasn't willing to pressure him. When the four talked with U Thant, the UN leader told them that he wasn't empowered to order such an inspection.[93]

In Washington, Kennedy sent the following reply to Khrushchev:

> I am replying at once to your broadcast message of October 28, even though the official text has not yet reached me, because of the great importance I attach to moving forward promptly to the settlement of the Cuban crisis. I think that you and I, with our heavy responsibilities for the maintenance of peace, were aware that developments were approaching a point where events could have become unmanageable. So I welcome this message and consider it an important contribution to peace.

---

[90] Schlesinger, *Robert Kennedy*, 565.
[91] Ibid.
[92] Brugioni, *Eyeball to Eyeball*, 571.
[93] Elie Abel, *The Missile Crisis* (Philadelphia and New York: J. B. Lippincott, 1986), 206-7.

The distinguished efforts of Acting Secretary-General U Thant have greatly facilitated both our tasks. I consider my letter to you of October 27 and your reply of today as firm undertakings on the part of both our governments which should be promptly carried out. I hope that the necessary measures can at once be taken through the United Nations as your message says, so that the United States in turn can remove the quarantine measures now in effect. I have already made arrangements to report all these matters to the Organization of American States, whose members share a deep interest in a genuine peace in the Caribbean area.

You referred in your letter to a violation of your frontier by an American aircraft in the area of the Chukotsk Peninsula. I have learned that this plane, without arms or photographic equipment, was engaged in an air sampling mission in connection with your nuclear tests. Its course was direct from Eiselson Air Force Base in Alaska to the North Pole and return. In turning south, the pilot made a serious navigational error which carried him over Soviet territory. He immediately made an emergency call on open radio for navigational assistance and was guided back to his home base by the most direct route. I regret this incident and will see to it that every precaution is taken to prevent recurrence.

Mr. Chairman, both of our countries have great unfinished tasks and I know that your people as well as those of the United States can ask for nothing better than to pursue them free from the fear of war. Modern science and technology have given us the possibility of making labor fruitful beyond anything that could have been dreamed of a few decades ago.

I agree with you that we must devote urgent attention to the problem of disarmament, as it relates to the whole world and also to critical areas. Perhaps now, as we step back from danger, we can together make real progress in this vital field. I think we should give priority to questions relating to the proliferation of nuclear weapons, on earth and in outer space, and to the great effort for a nuclear test ban. But we should also work hard to see if wider measures of disarmament can be agreed and put into operation at an early date. The United States government will be prepared to discuss these questions urgently, and in a constructive spirit, at Geneva or elsewhere.[94]

---

[94] Chang and Kornbluh, *The Cuban Missile Crisis, 1962*, 230-2.

Those two letters — from Khrushchev and Kennedy — ended the most dangerous stage of the crisis, but those who naively believed that the U.S. authorities would be satisfied soon learned that this was wishful thinking. In the same meeting on October 28 in which Kennedy's reply (reproduced above) was considered, it was decided to pressure the Soviets to withdraw the IL-28 bombers from Cuba, as well, for they were considered "offensive."

Fidel Castro learned of the Soviet Premier's offer and Kennedy's acceptance of Khrushchev's conditions at around midday. He was neither consulted nor even informed of the decision made in the Kremlin. The withdrawal of the missiles and the way that decision was made was a painful blow to both the Cuban government and people. Even though, looking back on events, it may be considered that war was averted, the problem had not been solved in a way that would remove the threat to Cuba. The Pentagon hawks and the most reactionary elements in Congress increased their pressures to launch an invasion of Cuba and bring about a thermonuclear war, and Cuba was left without any real guarantees that the United States wouldn't attempt an invasion at another time. Nor did the United States lift its naval and economic blockades of the island or suspend the flights of its spy planes, as was immediately shown.

In those circumstances, the Prime Minister of Cuba stated that a definitive solution of the crisis had not been reached and that there would be no guarantees to prevent an act of aggression against Cuba "unless, in addition to lifting the naval blockade, which he promises, President Kennedy also adopts the following five points:

1. The lifting of the economic blockade and the cessation of all the measures that the United States is taking all over the world to exert economic pressure against our country and hinder trade with it.
2. The cessation of all subversive activities, such as the launching and landing of weapons and explosives by air and by sea, the organization of mercenary invasions, and the infiltration of spies and saboteurs, all of which is being done from the territory of the United States and from that of some of its accomplices.
3. The cessation of the pirate attacks which are being carried out from bases in the United States and Puerto Rico.
4. The cessation of all violations of our airspace and territorial waters by U.S. planes and warships.

5. Withdrawal from the Guantánamo Naval Base (which the United States has occupied and operated since the turn of the century, when the compromised government of the time was forced to authorize this) and return of the Cuban territory occupied by the United States.[95]

All that Cuba proposed was respect for international law and the principles and provisions of the Charter of the United Nations. At that moment of U.S. saber rattling and Soviet weakness, however, none of this was achieved.

Thirty years later, in an interview for U.S. television, Fidel Castro commented that all that was needed was for Khrushchev to have said that he was ready to withdraw the missiles with guarantees that were satisfactory to Cuba. "Just a phrase would have been enough" to solve the crisis, "because nobody would have been willing to start a nuclear war over the Guantánamo Base, an economic blockade or an act of hostility against a small country. It would have been almost the same as the formula that was applied, but they should have added one phrase: We are willing to withdraw the missiles if the United States provides guarantees that are satisfactory to Cuba. Cuba should have been able to take part in that discussion and say which guarantees would be satisfactory to our country. Just one phrase would have been enough and would have changed that situation. After Khrushchev was willing to withdraw the missiles, nobody would have been willing to start a nuclear war over things that weren't important to the United States and the rest of the world, but which were very important to Cuba."[96]

---

[95] *Posición de Cuba ante la Crisis del Caribe* [Cuba's Position on the Caribbean Crisis]. Edited by the Commission of Revolutionary Orientation of the Integrated Revolutionary Organizations, Havana, December 1962.

[96] Maria Schriver, *Interview with Fidel Castro for NBC* (Havana: Editora Política, 1993). Translated from Spanish.

All times cited prior to October 28 are Daylight Savings Time, unless otherwise noted. On October 28, Daylight Savings Time changed to Eastern Standard Time. Note from *The Cuban Missile Crisis, 1962: A Chronology*, 1990, The National Security Archives, 33.

5

A misunderstanding

After sending his letter to Kennedy on October 28, Khrushchev wrote Fidel Castro of the agreement they had reached and about the downing of the U-2:

Dear Comrade Fidel Castro:
Our October 27 message to President Kennedy allows for the question to be settled in your favor, to defend Cuba from an invasion and prevent war from breaking out. Kennedy's reply, which you apparently also know, offers assurances that the United States will not invade Cuba with its own forces, nor will it permit its allies to carry out an invasion. In this way, the President of the United States has responded positively to my messages of October 26 and 27, 1962.

We have now finished drafting our reply to the President's message. I am not going to convey it here, for you surely know the text, which is now being broadcast over the radio.

With this motive I would like to recommend to you — at this moment of change in the crisis — not to be carried away by sentiment and to show firmness. I must say that I understand your feelings of indignation toward the aggression and violations of elementary norms of international law on the part of the United States.

But rather than law, what now prevails is the senselessness of the militarists at the Pentagon. Now that an agreement is within sight, the Pentagon is searching for a pretext to frustrate this agreement. This is why it is organizing the provocative flights. Yesterday you shot down one of these, while earlier you didn't shoot them down when they flew over your territory. The aggressors will take advantage of such a step for their own purposes.

Therefore, I would like to advise you in a friendly manner to show patience, firmness and even more firmness. Naturally, if there is an invasion it will be necessary to repulse it by every means. But we must not allow ourselves to be carried away by provocations. The Pentagon's unbridled militarists, now that the solution to the conflict is in sight and apparently in your favor — creating a guarantee against the invasion of Cuba — are trying to frustrate the agreement and provoke you into actions that could be used against you. I ask you not to give them the pretext for doing that.

On our part, we will do everything possible to stabilize the situation in Cuba, defend Cuba against invasion and assure you the possibilities for peacefully building a socialist society.

I send you greetings, extended to all your leadership group.

N. Khrushchev[97]

That same day, October 28, the Cuban Prime Minister replied to the Soviet Premier as follows:

Dear Comrade Khrushchev:
I have just received your letter.

The position of our government concerning your communication to us is embodied in the statement formulated today, whose text you surely know.

I wish to clear up something concerning the antiaircraft measures we adopted. You say: "Yesterday you shot down one of these [planes], while earlier you didn't shoot them down when they flew over your territory."

Earlier isolated violations were committed without a determined military purpose or without a real danger stemming from those flights.

This time that wasn't the case. There was the danger of a surprise attack on certain military installations. We decided not to

[97] *The Kennedy-Khrushchev-Castro Correspondence During the Cuban Missile Crisis.* Compiled by Peter Kornbluh for the Havana Conference on the Cuban Missile Crisis, January 9-12, 1992. The National Security Archives, Washington D.C., 1992.

sit back and wait for a surprise attack, with our detection radar turned off, when the potentially aggressive planes flying with impunity over the targets could destroy them totally. We didn't think we should allow that after all the efforts and expenses incurred and, in addition, because it would weaken us greatly — militarily and morally. For that reason, on October 24 the Cuban forces mobilized 50 antiaircraft batteries, our entire reserve then, to provide support to the Soviet forces. If we sought to avoid the risks of a surprise attack, it was necessary for Cuban artillery to have orders to shoot. The Soviet command can furnish you with additional reports of what happened to the plane that was shot down.

Earlier, airspace violations were carried out de facto and furtively. Yesterday the U.S. government tried to legitimize the privilege of violating our airspace at any hour of the day and night. We cannot accept that, as it would be tantamount to giving up our sovereignty. However, we agree that we must avoid an incident at this precise moment that could seriously harm the negotiations, so we will instruct the Cuban batteries not to open fire — but only for as long as the negotiations last and without revoking the declaration published yesterday about the decision to defend our airspace. It should also be taken into account that under the current tense conditions, incidents can take place accidently.

I also wish to inform you that we are in principle opposed to an inspection of our territory.

I very much appreciate the efforts you have made to keep the peace and we are absolutely in agreement with the need for struggling for that goal. If this is accomplished in a just, solid and definitive manner, it will be an inestimable service to humanity.

Fidel Castro[98]

In Washington, Ambassador Dobrynin and Robert Kennedy met twice — on October 29 and 30 — to discuss the missiles in Turkey. The Soviet representative stated that the agreement to withdraw them should be formalized in writing, but the U.S. officials refused to do this and said that the spoken promise that had been made was sufficient, reiterating that the missiles would be withdrawn in four or five months. Six months later, on April 25, 1963, the United States withdrew its missiles from both Turkey and Italy.

---

[98] Ibid.

On October 30, in the first of the 11 confidential messages between Kennedy and Khrushchev that the State Department declassified in 1992, the Soviet leader said that the naval blockade should be lifted, as agreed, before any attempt was made to inspect Soviet ships. He asked that the U.S. troops be pulled out of the Guantánamo Naval Base, since it was a useless drain on the budget of the United States, and he reminded the United States that the Soviet Union had closed down the bases it had in Finland and China. He urged that China's reincorporation into the United Nations be facilitated and stated that there could be no effective disarmament if China were not included. In addition, he touched on the problem of the withdrawal of troops from West Berlin and spoke of promoting the negotiations for signing a treaty on the prohibition of nuclear testing.

The news that reached the Kremlin from Havana wasn't pleasing, so Khrushchev wrote a letter to Fidel Castro that same day (October 30) in which he said that he didn't understand the message that the Cuban Prime Minister had sent him on October 28. Khrushchev tried to justify the fact that he had not consulted his ally about the withdrawal of the missiles:

Dear Comrade Fidel Castro:
We have received your letter of October 28 and the reports on the talks that you as well as President Dorticós have had with our ambassador.

We understand your situation and take into account the difficulties you now have after the diminishing of tension that arose from the threat of attack by U.S. imperialism, an attack which you expected would occur at any moment.

We understand that certain difficulties have been created for you as a result of our having promised the U.S. government to withdraw the missile base from Cuba, since it is viewed as an offensive weapon. This was in exchange for the U.S. commitment to abandon plans for an invasion of Cuba by U.S. troops or those of its allies in the western hemisphere, and lift the so-called "quarantine," that is, bring the blockade of Cuba to an end. This led to the resolution of the conflict in the Caribbean zone which, as you well realize, saw the clash of two superpowers and the possibility of it being transformed into a thermonuclear world war.

As we learned from our ambassador, some Cubans have the opinion that the Cuban people want a declaration of another kind rather than the declaration of the withdrawal of the missiles. It is possible that this kind of feeling exists among the people. But we, political and government figures, are leaders of a people who don't know everything and cannot readily comprehend all that we leaders must deal with. Therefore, we should march at the head of the people and then the people will follow us and respect us.

Had we, yielding to the sentiments prevailing among the people, allowed ourselves to be carried away by certain passionate sectors of the population and refused to come to a reasonable agreement with the U.S. government, then a war could have broken out. In the course of this war millions of people would have died and the survivors would have pinned the blame on the leaders for not having taken all the necessary measures to prevent that war of annihilation.

Preventing the war and an attack on Cuba depended not just on the measures adopted by our government but also on an estimate of the actions of the enemy forces deployed near you. Accordingly, the overall situation had to be considered.

In addition, there are opinions that you and we failed to take into consideration before adopting the decision known to you.

For this reason, we believe that we consulted with you, dear Comrade Fidel Castro. We received the cables, each one more alarming than the next, and finally your cable of October 27 saying you were nearly certain that an attack on Cuba would be launched. You believed that it was merely a question of time, that the attack would take place within the next 24 to 72 hours. Upon receiving this alarming cable from you and aware of your courage, we viewed it as a very well-founded alarm.

Wasn't this consultation on your part with us? I have viewed this cable as a signal of extreme alarm. We also had information that the unabated warmongering group of U.S. militarists wanted to take advantage of the situation that had been created and launch an attack on Cuba. Under the conditions created, if we had continued our consultations we would have wasted time and this attack would have been carried out.

We came to the conclusion that our strategic missiles in Cuba became an ominous force for the imperialists: they were frightened and because of their fear that our rockets could be launched, they could have dared to liquidate them by bombing them or launching an invasion of Cuba. And it must be said that they could have knocked them all out. Therefore, I repeat, your alarm was absolutely well-founded.

In your cable of October 27 you proposed that we be the first to launch a nuclear strike against the territory of the enemy. You, of course, realize where that would have led. Rather than a simple strike, it would have been the start of a thermonuclear world war.

Dear Comrade Fidel Castro, I consider this proposal of yours incorrect, although I understand your motivation.

We have lived through the most serious moment when a nuclear world war could have broken out. Obviously, in that case, the United States would have sustained huge losses, but the Soviet Union and the whole socialist camp would have also suffered greatly. As far as Cuba is concerned, it would be difficult to say even in general terms what this would have meant. In the first place, Cuba would have been engulfed in the fire of war. There is no doubt that the Cuban people would have fought courageously nor that they would have died heroically. But we are not struggling against imperialism in order to die, but to take advantage of all our possibilities, to lose less in the struggle and win more to overcome and achieve the victory of communism.

Now, as a result of the measures taken, we reached the goal sought when we initially agreed with you to send the missiles to Cuba. We have wrested from the United States the commitment not to invade Cuba and not to permit their Latin American allies to do so. We have wrested all this from them without a nuclear strike.

We consider that we must take advantage of all the possibilities to defend Cuba, strengthen its independence and sovereignty, defeat military aggression and prevent a nuclear world war in our time.

And we have accomplished that.

Of course, we made concessions, accepted a commitment, acting according to the principle that a concession on one side is answered by a concession on the other side. The United States also made a concession. It made the commitment before all the world not to attack Cuba.

That's why when we compare aggression on the part of the United States and thermonuclear war with the commitment to uphold the inviolability of the Republic of Cuba and the prevention of a world war, I think that the total outcome of this reckoning is perfectly clear.

Naturally, in defending Cuba as well as the other socialist countries we can't rely on a U.S. government veto. We have adopted and will continue to adopt in the future all the measures necessary to strengthen our defense and build up our forces, so that we can strike back if necessary. At present, as a result of weapons supplies, Cuba is stronger than ever. Even after the dismantling of the missile installations you will have powerful weapons to repel the enemy — on land, in the air and on the sea — in the approaches to the island. At the same time, as you will recall, we have said in our October 28 message to the President of the United States that we want to assure the Cuban people that we stand at their side and that we will not forget our responsibility to help the Cuban people. It is clear to everyone that this is an extremely important warning to the enemy on our part.

You also stated during the rallies that the United States can't be trusted. That, of course, is correct. We also view your statements on the conditions of the talks with the United States as correct. The shooting down of a U.S. plane over Cuba turned out to be a useful measure because this operation ended without complications. Let it be a lesson for the imperialists.

Needless to say, our enemies will interpret the events in their own way. The Cuban counterrevolution will also try to raise its head. But we think you will completely dominate your domestic enemies without our assistance. The main thing we have secured is preventing aggression on the part of your foreign enemy at present.

We feel that the aggressor came out the loser. It made preparations to attack Cuba but was stopped by us and forced to recognize before world public opinion that it won't attack at this stage. We view this as a great victory. The imperialists, of course, will not stop their struggle against communism. But we also have our plans and we are going to adopt our measures. This process of struggle will continue as long as there are two political and social systems in the world, until one of these — and we know it will be our communist system — wins and triumphs throughout the world.

Comrade Fidel Castro, I have decided to send this reply to you as soon as possible. A more detailed analysis of everything that has happened will be made in the letter I will send you shortly. In that letter I will make the broadest analysis of the situation and give you my evaluation of the outcome of the conflict.

Now, as the talks to settle the conflict get underway, I ask you to send me your considerations. For our part, we will continue to report to you on the development of these talks and make all necessary consultations.

I wish you success, Comrade Fidel Castro. You will no doubt have success. There will be machinations against you, but together with you we will adopt all the measures necessary to neutralize them and contribute to the strengthening and development of the Cuban revolution.

N. Khrushchev[99]

The same day on which he wrote this letter and the next day, when Fidel Castro replied to it, the Secretary-General of the United Nations was in Havana to talk with members of the Cuban government, as requested by the Security Council. Those talks were quite interesting, concerning the on-site inspections which the United States demanded, among other things.

On October 31, in replying to Khrushchev, the Cuban leader said that he hadn't suggested a first strike and that he hadn't been consulted about the withdrawal of the missiles:

Dear Comrade Khrushchev:

I received your letter of October 30. You believe that we were consulted before you adopted the decision to withdraw the strategic missiles. You base yourself on the alarming news that you say reached you from Cuba and, finally, my cable of October 27. I don't know what news you received; I can only respond for the message that I sent you on the evening of October 26, which reached you on October 27.

What we did in the face of the events, Comrade Khrushchev, was to prepare ourselves and get ready to fight. In Cuba there was only one kind of alarm, that of battle stations.

When in our opinion the imperialist attack became imminent, I deemed it appropriate to so advise you and to alert the Soviet government and command — since there were Soviet forces committed to fight at our side to defend the Republic of Cuba from foreign aggression — about the possibility of an attack which we could not prevent but could resist.

I told you that the morale of our people was very high and that the aggression would be heroically resisted. At the end of the message I reiterated to you that we awaited the events calmly.

Danger couldn't overwhelm us, because danger has been hanging over our country for a long time now and in a certain way we have grown used to it.

---

[99] Ibid.

The Soviet troops who have been at our side know how admirable the stand of our people was throughout this crisis and the profound fraternity that was created among the troops from both peoples during the decisive hours. Countless Cubans and Soviets who were willing to die with supreme dignity shed tears upon learning about the surprising, sudden and practically unconditional decision to withdraw the weapons.

Perhaps you don't know the degree to which the Cuban people were ready to carry out its duty to the nation and humanity.

I realized when I wrote them that the words contained in my letter could be misinterpreted by you and that was what happened — perhaps because you didn't read them carefully, perhaps because of the translation, perhaps because I meant to say so much in too few lines. However, I didn't hesitate to do it. Do you believe, Comrade Khrushchev, that we were selfishly thinking of ourselves, of our generous people willing to sacrifice themselves, and not in an unconscious manner but fully aware of the risk they ran?

No, Comrade Khrushchev. Few times in history, and it could even be said that never before — because no people had ever faced such a tremendous danger — was a people so willing to fight and die with such a universal sense of duty.

We knew — and do not presume that we ignored it, as you insinuate in your letter — that we would have been annihilated in the event of nuclear war. However, that didn't prompt us to ask you to withdraw the missiles, that didn't prompt us to ask you to yield. Do you believe that we wanted war? But how could we prevent it if the invasion finally took place? The fact is that this event was possible, that imperialism was obstructing every solution and that its demands were, from our point of view, impossible for the Soviet Union and Cuba to accept.

And if war had broken out, what could we do with the insane people who unleashed the war? You yourself have said that under current conditions such a war would inevitably have escalated quickly into a nuclear war.

I understand that once aggression is unleashed, one shouldn't concede to the aggressor the privilege of deciding when to use nuclear weapons. The destructive power of this weaponry is so great and the speed of its delivery so swift that the aggressor would have a considerable initial advantage.

And I did not suggest to you, Comrade Khrushchev, that the Soviet Union should be the aggresor, because that would not only have been incorrect, it would be immoral and contemptible on my part. But from the instant the imperialists attack Cuba and while there are Soviet armed forces stationed in Cuba to help in our defense in case of an attack from abroad, the imperialists would by this act become aggressors against Cuba and against the Soviet Union, and we would respond with a strike that would annihilate them.

Everyone has their own opinions, and I maintain mine about the danger of the aggressive circles in the Pentagon and their preference for a preemptive strike. I did not suggest, Comrade Khrushchev, that in the midst of this crisis the Soviet Union should attack, which is what your letter seems to say; rather, that following an imperialist attack, the Soviet Union should act without vacillation and should never make the mistake of allowing circumstances to develop in which the enemy makes the first nuclear strike against the Soviet Union. And in this sense, Comrade Khrushchev, I maintain my point of view, because I understand it to be a true and just evaluation of a specific situation. You may be able to convince me that I am wrong, but you can't tell me that I am wrong without convincing me.

I know that this is a delicate issue that can only be broached in circumstances such as these and in a very personal message.

You may wonder what right I have to broach this topic. I do so without worrying about how thorny it is, following the dictates of my conscience as a revolutionary and inspired by the most unselfish sentiments of admiration and affection for the Soviet Union, for what it represents for the future of humanity and by the concern that it should never again be the victim of the perfidy and betrayal of aggressors, as it was in 1941, which cost so many lives and so much destruction. Moreover, I spoke not as a troublemaker but as a combatant from the most endangered trenches.

I do not see how you can state that we were consulted in the decision you took.

I would like nothing more than to be proved wrong at this moment. I only wish that you were right.

There are not just a few Cubans, as has been reported to you, but in fact many Cubans who are experiencing at this moment unspeakable bitterness and sadness.

The imperialists are talking once again of invading our country, which is proof of how ephemeral and untrustworthy their promises are. Our people, however, maintain their indestructible will to resist the aggressors and perhaps more than ever need to trust in themselves and in that will to struggle.

We will struggle against adverse circumstances, we will overcome the current difficulties and we will come out ahead, and nothing can destroy the ties of friendship and the eternal gratitude we feel toward the Soviet Union.

Fraternally,

Fidel Castro[100]

The war against Cuba continued. On October 30, a pirate vessel attacked the southern part of Caleta del Humo, a town in the western province of Pinar del Río. The counterrevolutionaries who tried to enter the country undetected were arrested. That same day, there was another attack, from the sea, against Mambí Cay, off the northern coast of Oriente Province. On November 5, the head of the CIA's Cuban Special Missions Group was captured together with another agent, while engaging in sabotage against the copper mines in Pinar del Río Province. On November 14, individuals who had entered the country illegally in the southern part of the city of Santiago de Cuba were arrested. On November 19, a pirate vessel attacked the Jagua area of the city of Cienfuegos, in the south-central part of the country. On November 20, planes with U.S. registration tried to sink the Cuban merchant vessel *Damují*. On December 1, some individuals entered the country illegally just east of the town of Rosario on the southern coast of Havana Province. On December 6, a vessel from the United States attacked a fishermen's hamlet on the northern coast of Las Villas Province. On December 8, a pirate vessel attacked the port of Caibarién. On December 21, a U.S. military intelligence agent paid a Canadian to introduce a disease in Cuba that was injurious to turtles. That wound up the covert operations of 1962. [101]

---

[100] Ibid.

[101] Fabián Escalante Font, *The Secret War: The CIA's Covert Operations Against Cuba 1959-62* (Melbourne: Ocean Press, 1995).

6

U Thant in Havana

I n 1962, as in all other years, a concert was held in the General Assembly hall on October 24 to mark United Nations Day. While the orchestra played, Secretary-General U Thant wrote messages to the Soviet Premier and the U.S. President in his office on the 38th floor of the UN building. He asked the former to stop sending weapons to Cuba and the latter to lift the naval blockade for two or three weeks to make it possible to find a peaceful solution to the conflict. He also appealed to the Cuban President and Prime Minister, asking them to stop building launching pads for the nuclear weapons while negotiations were held.

He received replies to his letters the next day. Khrushchev accepted without any strings attached and expressed the need for UN intervention, "in view of the seriousness of the situation." Kennedy said that his ambassador to the United Nations would discuss any agreement, but he warned that the threat had been created by the secret introduction of offensive weapons in Cuba, and that the only solution was to have those weapons withdrawn. Some hours later, U Thant again communicated with the White House and the Kremlin, expressing his concern that the Soviet ships on their way to Cuba might challenge the U.S. blockade, bringing about a clash that would destroy all possibility of negotiation. He urged Khrushchev to order his ships to remain away from the line of interception for a limited time, and asked Kennedy to ensure that his ships would do everything possible to avoid a direct confrontation. Khrushchev agreed, and so did Kennedy, but Kennedy warned that the matter to be negotiated was urgent, since work on the missile installations hadn't stopped.

On October 26, the UN Secretary-General informed Fidel Castro of Khrushchev's and Kennedy's replies to his messages and told him that he could make a significant contribution to world peace by ordering the suspension of construction work on the bases while the negotiations — which were about to begin — were held. The next day, the Cuban Prime Minister replied that his country was willing to discuss its differences with the United States and to do everything in its power to cooperate with the United Nations to end the crisis, but that it could not accept the naval blockade, which violated Cuba's sovereignty and which he described as an act of force and war imposed by the United States. He also rejected the U.S. presumption that it could decide what Cuba had or had not the right to do in its own territory, the kind of weapons it might use for its defense, whether or not it could have relations with the Soviet Union and what steps it could take in its international policy to guarantee its security and sovereignty. He added that the Cuban government would be willing to accept the pledges U Thant was requesting as efforts toward peace — if, at the same time, the U.S. government would stop its threats and aggressive actions against Cuba, including the naval blockade, in the period of negotiations. At the end of his letter, he invited U Thant to visit Havana to discuss the crisis. U Thant accepted the invitation on October 29.

The crisis had taken another turn. While these messages were being exchanged, the Soviet Union had already decided to withdraw the missiles, and, on October 28, Fidel Castro demanded five guarantees so the White House would keep its promise of not invading Cuba.

Shortly after midday on October 30, the UN Secretary-General arrived at Havana's airport with a large entourage of international officials. The U.S. press and its allies, which either refused to print or distorted Cuba's statements, rather unsubtly stated that U Thant was going to Cuba to force it to accept UN inspections. The Burmese diplomat was worried that those distorted interpretations would hamper his efforts in Havana and he denied the reports (obviously aimed at pressuring him) before getting on his plane in New York. U Thant stated that in responding to the invitation issued by Fidel Castro, he intended to discuss all of the important aspects of the problem so as to reach a solution that would affirm the principle of respect for Cuban sovereignty.

After landing in Cuba, U Thant was taken to the Presidential Palace where Prime Minister Fidel Castro, President Osvaldo Dorticós, Foreign Minister Raúl Roa and myself (who had been named Cuban ambassador to the United Nations) awaited him. U Thant was accompanied by Omar Loufti, of Egypt, and Hernane Tavares de Saa, of Brazil, both Under Secretaries-General, and by Brigadier General Indar J. Rikhye, of India, U Thant's military adviser, who had kept him informed in the preceding days about the rumors that were circulating in Washington.

No U.S. diplomats had warned the Secretary-General of the crisis that was approaching. General Rikhye informed U Thant on Saturday, October 20, that there was irrefutable proof of the presence of Soviet missiles in Cuba, which Philip Dean, the United Nations representative in the U.S. capital, confirmed by telephone the same day. On Monday morning, Rikhye had told U Thant that President Kennedy was preparing an important statement and advised him to call in Ambassador Stevenson to talk about it. By the time Stevenson arrived in U Thant's office, the White House's announcement had already gone out over the radio.[102] A few days later, Rikhye told the Secretary-General that there were around 30 missiles in Cuba but that he didn't believe they would be ready to be activated until new supplies arrived from the Soviet Union.[103] That was the news that the future mediator from the United Nations had at that time.

On taking a seat in the conference hall of the Presidential Palace in Havana along with his two Under Secretaries, U Thant asked Fidel Castro if General Rikhye might take part in the talks, and Fidel Castro agreed. U Thant began the dialogue by saying that while the Security Council was in session the representatives of 45 nonaligned countries had met and asked him to take the initiative to find a peaceful solution, which is why he had sent messages to the leaders of the three countries involved. He said that, as he viewed the problem at that time, there were two parts to the question: one immediate and the other long term. He stated that the negotiations that he had begun with the three powers were on the immediate problem but that the United Nations would have to take part in finding a long-term solution, as well.

He said that the United States wanted to establish a United Nations mechanism to guarantee that no more weapons would enter Cuba starting three weeks from then and noted that the Soviet Union

---

[102] U Thant, *View from the UN* (London: David and Charles, Newton Abbot, 1977), 155.
[103] Ibid., 161.

had agreed to that proposal. Later on, the Soviet Union stated that the inspections should be made by the Red Cross, which said it would do this, either on the high seas or at the ports where the cargos were to be unloaded, only if the Cuban government agreed. The Secretary-General said that he didn't associate himself with any of the proposals. He said that he had informed the conflicting powers that the most important thing was to obtain the Cuban government's prior consent and that no actions which infringed on its sovereignty could be taken.

U Thant said that, if the proposal of a UN inspection was accepted, Washington would issue a statement in the Security Council pledging not to invade Cuba and would lift the blockade, and he repeated what he had stated in the Security Council — that a naval blockade was an unusual action which shouldn't be resorted to except in times of war. He said that the representatives of the 45 nonaligned countries shared that point of view and that the representatives of other nonaligned countries, especially those represented at the Belgrade Conference, would make similar statements if given the opportunity to do so.

Fidel Castro then asked for details about the inspection formulas. U Thant said that there would be two inspection units: one on land and the other in the air. They were to function until the bases had been dismantled. Fidel Castro said that he didn't understand why those things were being requested. U Thant replied that the United States wanted to be sure that the bases were really being dismantled and that the missiles were returned to the Soviet Union.[104]

> *Fidel Castro* — What right does the the United States have to ask this? I mean, is this based on an actual right, or is it a demand by force, dictated from a position of strength?
>
> *U Thant* — This is my point of view: It is not a right. Something such as this could only take place with the approval and acceptance of the Cuban government.
>
> *Fidel Castro* — We do not know precisely why this is asked of us, because we have not violated any law, we have not carried out any act of aggression against anyone. All our actions have been based on international law; we have done absolutely nothing outside of the norms of international law. On the other hand, we

---

[104] Interview between UN Secretary-General U Thant, and his delegation, with the Prime Minister of the Revolutionary Government, Dr. Fidel Castro Ruz; the President, Dr. Osvaldo Dorticós; Cuban Foreign Minister, Dr. Raul Roa; and Dr. Carlos Lechuga, Cuban ambassador to Mexico. Presidential Palace, Havana, Cuba, first session, October 30, 1962. Translated from Spanish, 9-11.

have been the victims, firstly, of a blockade that is an illegal act; and secondly, of the interference of another country in what we have a right to do or not do within our own borders.

We understand Cuba to be a sovereign state no more or less so than any other of the member states of the United Nations, and with all the attributes inherent to any of these states.

Furthermore, the United States has repeatedly violated our airspace without any right to do so, thus carrying out an intolerable act of aggression against our country. They have attempted to justify this with a resolution of the Organization of American States, but for us this OAS resolution lacks any validity. We were in fact also expelled from the OAS.

We can accept anything that conforms to law, that does not cost us our sovereignty. The rights violated by the United States have not been restored, and we do not accept any imposition through force.

I know that this issue of the inspection is a further attempt to humiliate our country. Therefore, we do not accept it.

These demands for an inspection aim to violate our right to act within our borders with total freedom, to decide what we can or cannot do within our borders...

We are willing to negotiate with complete sincerity and integrity. We would not be worthy if we were willing to negotiate the sovereignty of our country. We are prepared to pay any price to defend that sovereignty.[105]

U Thant said that his conscience was clear on this aspect and that the United Nations could only undertake an action of that kind with the consent of the government involved. He added that it wasn't the first time this had happened: when a situation arose in Laos that threatened international peace, the United Nations went in after obtaining the consent of the Lao government. In 1956, a similar situation arose in the United Arab Republic, and the United Nations went in there, too — again, with the consent of the government. Likewise, in Lebanon in 1958.[106]

Fidel Castro interrupted, pointing out that the Congo was another such case. U Thant remarked that it was also the case in Somalia. Fidel Castro exclaimed ironically, "In the Congo, the government that

---

[105] Ibid., 11-14.
[106] Ibid., 15.

requested it has since been buried,"[107] adding that, in all the cases mentioned, a series of attacks was made on the people's rights. "The same thing began it all," he said, "the road leading to the last World War started with German imperialism's annexation of Austria and occupation of Czechoslovakia, and we are aware of those dangers. We know the roads the aggressors like to take and we can see the road the United States wants to take regarding us." Therefore, he said, "It is really hard to understand how anyone can speak of immediate solutions independently of long-term solutions, when the most important thing is not to pay any price for peace, but to guarantee a definitive peace and not keep on paying the price of an ephemeral peace every day. Of course, Cuba isn't Austria, southeastern Czechoslovakia or the Congo. We are determined to defend our rights no matter what the difficulties, no matter what the risks." [108]

U Thant commented that the immediate and long-term solutions were very closely linked, and that the possibilities for achieving long-term solutions should be explored in light of the situation as it was then. In practice, it was very difficult to separate the two things. He said that he agreed with Fidel Castro's comments on Laos and the other cases in which the United Nations had gone in, but he also wanted to say that the United Nations had managed to stave off or avoid attack from abroad in those places. He then asked that the Cuban government consider the possibility of having the United Nations come in for perhaps a little more than three weeks, as it might stave off or eliminate the danger of an attack.

He said that he thought the short-term agreements should include negotiations for a long-term solution and that representatives of the United Nations should participate in the efforts to obtain it — which he believed would be difficult to attain at that time.

Fidel Castro then said that the reason a short-term solution hadn't been reached was because the United States didn't want one and was hell-bent on making inspections in Cuba; he pointed out that, for the purposes of the unilateral security it demanded, the Soviet government's decision to withdraw the strategic weapons should be enough, and the Cuban government hadn't raised any obstacles to the withdrawal of the weapons. The Soviet government's decision, he said, was a political one, and the United States knew that the weapons were being withdrawn.

---

[107] Ibid., 16.
[108] Ibid., 16-17.

U Thant repeated that the United States would make a public statement of non-aggression once the missiles had been withdrawn. Fidel Castro indicated that he was opposed to a Red Cross inspection in Cuban ports and asked why, if the Soviet Union had authorized its ships to be inspected on the high seas, it was necessary to inspect them again in Cuban ports. As for the statement that the United States wouldn't invade Cuba, he said that the United States had no right to attack his country and that it wasn't possible to negotiate with a promise not to commit a crime. Moreover, if the United Nations placed such high value on a public promise to it that one country wouldn't invade another, why didn't it place equal value on the Soviet Union's public promise to the United Nations that it would withdraw the strategic weapons? Both were public promises and if one of them — that of not invading Cuba — didn't need any additional guarantees, why did the Soviet Union's promise to withdraw the weapons need the additional guarantee of the inspections?

After the meeting, U Thant went to the residence that had been provided for him and talked first with Luis Bastián Pinto, the Brazilian ambassador to Cuba, and then with Soviet Ambassador Alexander Alexeev and General Igor D. Statenko, head of the missile division, who told him that the preparations for dismantling the launching pads were being completed.

The second meeting in the Presidential Palace took place the following morning. On his request, U Thant went alone. The first thing he mentioned was a letter that Khrushchev had sent Kennedy, agreeing to having UN observers verify that the missile installations were being dismantled. U Thant asked what the Cuban government thought about this, and the Prime Minister replied, "We understood, when the Soviet government decided to dismantle the bases and spoke of verification, that it meant some kind of inspection outside Cuban territory, since the Prime Minister of the Soviet Union couldn't speak of verification in Cuban territory, because that is a matter that only concerns the Revolutionary Government of Cuba."[109]

U Thant then expressed some of his own views. He said that there were three forces in the United States — the Pentagon, the Central Intelligence Agency and the State Department — and that, in his opinion, the Pentagon and the CIA were more powerful than the State Department. He said that if the CIA and the Pentagon continued to be as powerful as they then were, he didn't see much of a future for the world. He stated that both the blockade and the spy flights were illegal.

---

[109] Ibid., second session, October 31, 1962, 2.

U Thant — No state can impose a military blockade, not even an economic blockade. That is the imposition of the strength of a great power against a small country...

These three things — economic blockade, military blockade and spy flights — are illegal, and I told them so privately on Friday...

I told the United States that if they did something drastic, then not only would I report it to the Security Council, but that I would accuse the United States in the Security Council. Although the United States has votes and veto power, there can be, nevertheless, a moral sanction.

I also told them that I would resign from my position; that if the United Nations cannot stop the aggression of a great power against a small country, then I do not want to be Secretary-General.

I have not taken a single Sunday's rest; my family is very unhappy because I have so much work. If I cannot achieve peace then I have no reason to occupy the position.

On Saturday I repeated this once more to the United States, and I warned them not to carry out any act of aggression against Cuba for this would spell the end of the United Nations. . .

I would like to tone down the reports before the Security Council, in order to lessen the tension. In the United States, as you know, there is much hysteria; the press and radio stations are fostering this climate and I believe that the hysteria has to be lessened...[110]

As for what he called the long-term solution, he said that he had met for a long time the day before with the Brazilian ambassador to Cuba and General Albino Silva, who accompanied him, and added:

I have reached the conclusion that the best solution is not to solely concentrate on the immediate problem, but to look at the problem in the long term. I am totally convinced that this is the only solution: dealing with both problems at the same time. Thus I will inform the Security Council that if it does not deal, at the correct time, with the long-term problem, then it will not solve the crisis... The long-term discussion will face obstacles in the Security Council, due to the attitude of the United States...[111]

---

[110] Ibid., 3-4.
[111] Ibid., 8.

Fidel Castro commented that there would be no definitive solution if the five point guarantees that Cuba stipulated weren't met: "We are willing to search for definitive solutions and to solve the crisis permanently, but we won't accept a solution for the crisis under conditions that imply any kind of special status for our country or that doesn't preserve all of our country's sovereignty. It would be easy for us to accept an honorable agreement, because we don't have any conflicts with anybody or any aggressive intentions."[112]

U Thant said that he would report to the Security Council within a few days and that, if the discussions were kept outside that body, it would not intervene in them. He said that it would be better to wait until after the U.S. elections, because many delegations understood that a large part of the problem was caused by electoral considerations and that things would be discussed on a better footing after the voting. Later, he asked what had happened to the pilot of the plane that had been shot down and was told that he had died.

U Thant wanted to clarify whether or not Cuba insisted that the discussions be based only on the five points Fidel Castro had stipulated, and Fidel Castro replied that those points were so reasonable that none of them could be renounced. "It is very logical, elementary," he added, "that, if our friends' weapons leave Cuba, our enemies' weapons shouldn't remain in our territory. The United States says that the Guantánamo Naval Base is here by virtue of a treaty and acknowledges that a Cuban administration had the power to enter into that treaty. Why then, doesn't another Cuban administration have the right, by virtue of a treaty, to authorize bases in our national territory?... It can't accept weapons from its friends. As a matter of principle, we want all bases in foreign territories to disappear."[113]

Taking a very personal tone, U Thant said that being Secretary-General was a thankless task and that he had wanted to resign several times, but his friends had urged him to continue in his post, for the good of the future of the United Nations. He said that his mandate would expire in April but that, unfortunately, there weren't any other candidates. He stated that the week before he had again said he wanted to resign, but that he was the candidate acceptable to everyone, both the big powers and the nonaligned nations. He added that he had been away from his country for close to six years and had managed to

[112] Ibid., 9.
[113] Ibid., 15.

visit it for only 10 days in all that time. He concluded: "My wife is not happy in the United States."[114]

At the end of the meeting, he said he was convinced that many people in the United States didn't support that country's policy on Cuba, "in spite of the poisonous campaign of the press, radio and daily propaganda."[115]

He said that the day after he made his report to the Security Council he had received 620 telegrams from U.S. citizens asking the United Nations to solve the problem of Cuba peacefully and five asking that the United Nations stay out of the negotiations so the United States could invade the island. "On Monday, I received 200 cables, most of them calling for a peaceful solution to the Cuban problem."[116]

U Thant arrived back in New York on the evening of that same day, October 31. He returned with all of the UN personnel who had accompanied him; in the last meeting he had asked if he might leave one or two people whom he trusted in Havana to maintain direct contacts with the Cuban government. Fidel Castro told him that even though he would like to grant his request, he could not do so because the people might consider them to be some kind of inspectors. In any case, he added, U Thant would have contacts with the head of the Cuban diplomatic mission or with the Cuban Foreign Minister, who would travel to New York if necessary.

In New York, the Secretary-General found the same anti-Cuba hate campaign in the press as had been waged before he left, but with some new ingredients, such as the demand that the IL-28 bombers and Komar torpedo boats also be removed from Cuba — plus, of course, new threats about what would happen if Cuba didn't agree to on-site inspections.

It was in that political climate, whipped up by the mass media toeing Washington's official line, that the negotiators from the three countries — Adlai Stevenson and John McCloy (the U.S. representative in the disarmament negotiations with the Soviet Union) for the United States, Vasili Kuznetsov for the Soviet Union and myself for Cuba — began our talks. It was a very unique form of diplomacy in the history of international relations. Of the three protagonists in the crisis, only two countries negotiated with each other; one of those two discussed things with the third. Moreover all three — nearly always individually

---

[114] Ibid., 18.
[115] Ibid., 19.
[116] Ibid., 19.

— maintained contacts with the Secretary-General of the United Nations, even though the main issues were discussed outside the United Nations.

The day after his return to New York from Havana, U Thant met with Anastas Mikoyan, who was in New York on his way to Cuba. Khrushchev had given the Soviet Deputy Premier the difficult task of explaining to Fidel Castro why he had withdrawn the missiles in the way he had, without consulting Cuba, and why he had agreed to having inspectors verify the dismantling of the bases and the return of the missiles — also without consulting Cuba — all of which had clearly endangered relations between the two countries.

That evening, Mikoyan had dinner with Stevenson and McCloy, who rather incredibly "forgot" — or so they said — to give him the list of weapons that, in addition to the nuclear ballistic missiles, Kennedy demanded be withdrawn from Cuba. They didn't send the document to him until he was at the airport the next day, minutes before boarding the plane that was to take him to Havana, and Mikoyan indignantly refused to accept it.

The list of weapons that Washington considered offensive included the following: ground-to-ground missiles, including those designed to be used at sea, plus chemical compounds and fuel that could be used for supplying energy to the missiles; bombers; bombs, air-to-ground missiles and guided missiles; and nuclear warheads for any of those weapons and mechanical or electronic equipment for raising the weapons or making them functional — that is, communications equipment, energy supply equipment for launching the missiles and Komar torpedo boats. The appetite of the U.S. authorities was insatiable. At the end of the negotiations, however, they didn't insist on the withdrawal of the Komar torpedo boats.

On November 1, the day before Mikoyan arrived in Cuba, work began on dismantling the missile bases, and the missiles started on their journey back to the Soviet Union on Soviet ships a week later. The Cuban people's frustration was deep and vociferous; the Soviets who were in Cuba, risking their lives, also felt bitter about what Moscow had done. General Gribkov — who, as already noted, was head of the Main Operations Department and was in Cuba to see that the missions assigned to the troops from his country were carried out — stated in the 1992 meeting held in Cuba to analyze the crisis that the Soviet military officers felt very disillusioned by the withdrawal of the missiles and that he, who had fought in World War II as a tank lieutenant and had experienced both victory and defeat, considered the most humiliating experience in his 54 years in the military was the inspection of the Soviet ships at sea by U.S. ships and planes. The crew members of the Soviet ships had to take the canvas covers off the missiles when the U.S. authorities asked them to, so photographs could be taken from U.S. planes or ships. The Soviet negotiators in New York, Kuznetsov and Ambassador Zorin, had informed their U.S. counterparts of the dates the ships would leave the Cuban ports.

7

Cuba and the negotiations

The matter of inspections in Cuba was always on the agenda during the negotiations, because Washington kept hoping it could force the revolutionary government to agree to them. After his visit to the Cuban capital, U Thant sent a message to the International Committee of the Red Cross (ICRC) in Geneva through Pier Pascuale Spinelli, Under Secretary-General of the United Nations, asking if, after all of the concerned parties had been consulted, the Red Cross might consider the appointment of inspectors who would check the cargo of the Soviet ships. This message reached Switzerland on November 2, but the Geneva-based institution had already taken the matter up on October 29, having heard from New York that it might be asked to contribute.

A plenary session of the ICRC was held on October 31 and November 1, in which different views were expressed: some of the members said that this wasn't the role of the Red Cross, which should limit itself to helping the victims of a conflict; while others said that, while that was the Red Cross's role, the action under consideration could be described as an effort for peace. At the end of the deliberations, it was decided that it was too early to make a final decision and that the best thing would be, as a first step, to send a mission to New York and act on the outcome of the consultations.

The mission was composed of Paul Ruegger, former President of the International Committee of the Red Cross, and Melchior Borsinger, adviser to the ICRC. They weren't clear about the responsibility assigned them in U Thant's note — whether the inspectors were to come from outside the institution or be officials of it. Reflecting the ICRC's discussions in Geneva, they thought it would be more correct for a commission of the United Nations to carry out the task — or, if the ICRC had to do it, the three countries directly involved — Cuba, the United States and the Soviet Union — should give the inspectors a mandate to that effect before they started work. The delegates remained in New York from November 6 through 11, while the Executive Council of the ICRC met in Geneva on November 8 to take up the matter again; the previous discussions were repeated.

The mission's first contacts were with the Secretary-General; Under Secretaries-General Omar Lufti and Ralph Bunche; General Rikhye; and Constantin Stavropoulos, UN legal counsel. Later, in the anteroom to U Thant's office, the members of the mission talked with Admiral Charles Youst and Vice-Admiral Wellborn, of the United States, Platon Morosov, Ambassador of the Soviet Union, and, lastly, with me, representing Cuba. After this, they met again with U Thant, who was accompanied by Chakravanthi Narashima, his head of staff, and with the Security Council adviser. Some days later, they met with Kuznetsov, Zorin, Stevenson and McCloy. On November 7, they met with me again, and, on November 8, the government of Cuba informed U Thant and the International Committee of the Red Cross that it wouldn't take any stand on the matter if the inspections were carried out on the high seas. The last meeting was with the Secretary-General on November 10. Simultaneously with those contacts, the UN Secretariat prepared a draft in conjunction with the ICRC.

Ruegger and Borsinger went back to Geneva and reported to the ICRC on their efforts on November 12, and the next day a communiqué was issued stating that the ICRC's task would consist mainly in appointing a team of inspectors who would act under the authority of the United Nations; the ICRC would not assume responsibility for the action; and the instructions that the United Nations would issue would be in line with the principles of the Red Cross, in the understanding that the prior consent of the three interested governments was required. In the end, no agreement was reached.

Those efforts were made and the discussions were held after Cuba had announced that it would not submit to any inspection, but that if inspections were made on the high seas beyond the area where it exercised its sovereignty, it wouldn't take any position on the matter. It is hard to understand — and this was never made clear — why the Red Cross, the United Nations, the United States and the Soviet Union kept insisting during those first few days of November on using the ICRC and the United Nations to check that the weapons were shipped out and on seeking Cuba's consent for these inspections.

The Congressional election was held in the United States on November 6, with victory for the Democratic Party's candidates, to Kennedy's great satisfaction. The demand for on-site inspections continued in force. This was now done not for the purpose of winning the election but in order to freeze the promise of not invading Cuba, making it conditional on Cuba's allowing inspections in its territory. No matter how the U.S. negotiators approached the issue, the only thing they could not do was force the Cuban government to accept the presence of inspectors in its territory.

Certainly, Washington's only purpose was to humiliate Cuba; this was clearly shown in Kennedy's reply to a question that his friend Ben Bradlee, of *Newsweek* magazine, asked him in the White House on November 15: "How was he sure the Russians weren't taking out old telephone poles instead of missiles under those canvas covers that appeared on the decks of the Soviet ships in the intelligence pictures? Kennedy admitted they had never seen those missiles without the covers... but he emphasized that it really made little difference. If the Soviets did not take the missiles out, this would become known sooner or later, and the Russians knew for sure that that would mean an immediate and massive invasion of Cuba by the United States to get the missiles out."[117] He also said that they assumed no missiles remained in caves — at least no medium- or intermediate-range missiles — and that "this assumption is based primarily on the evidence he has of their removal, plus their conviction that both Khrushchev and Castro know the United States will invade [Cuba] if any offensive missiles are found."[118]

U Thant stated in his memoirs that it was the Russians who had suggested using the Red Cross. He recalled that when Kuznetsov met with him the first time he said that, even though Moscow did not object to having the United Nations send a team of observers to confirm the dismantling of the launching pads in Cuba, his government would rather have the Red Cross do this, if Cuba agreed, and U Thant passed this on to Stevenson, who replied that he thought his government would accept this.

---

[117] Benjamin Bradlee, *Conversations with Kennedy* (New York: Pocket Books, 1976), 114 and 115.
[118] Ibid., 115.

Later on, another change was made to the idea of verification, this time at the initiative of U Thant, who sent a confidential letter to Fidel Castro on November 12 suggesting that he invite a group of ambassadors from Asian, African, European and Latin American countries who were accredited in Cuba to inspect the removal of the missiles. In the letter, the Secretary-General reminded Fidel Castro that he knew from their talks that he was very concerned about peace, but not peace at any price, and never at the expense of his country's sovereignty, which was why he opposed intervention by the United Nations — but that he was suggesting that formula, even so.

The Cuban leader replied that he appreciated the great efforts the Secretary-General was making to protect humanity from the catastrophic risks of a nuclear war and that he, too, wanted to safeguard world peace, but not at any price. He had given careful study to the proposal that a group of ambassadors verify the removal of the strategic weapons, even though those weapons had already been withdrawn at the decision of the Soviet government. However, Cuba stood firm by its decision not to allow any kind of inspection within its territory, for any such inspection would imply an infringement of his government's and the Cuban people's inalienable right to make sovereign decisions on everything within Cuba's internal jurisdiction, especially its national defense against direct or indirect attack by a foreign power.

For his part, Fidel Castro suggested that those Latin American, African, Asian and European countries attempt to find a permanent solution for the situation — one which would, of course, include a discussion of the five points that Cuba considered to be minimal guarantees for the preservation of its self-determination, independence and sovereignty. At the end of his November 14 letter in reply to U Thant, Fidel Castro said that, even though the strategic defense weapons had been removed, the illegal blockade of Cuba, the violations of its airspace and the acts of provocation from the Guantánamo Naval Base continued.

As soon as the Secretary-General had returned from Cuba, the Soviet and Cuban negotiators began to draw up a draft protocol that the three countries would submit to the Security Council. As noted, the talks were carried out between the Soviet and U.S. negotiators on the one hand and between the Soviet and Cuban negotiators on the other, plus the representatives of each country, separately, with U Thant. Edwin Martin, who was Assistant Secretary of State for Inter-American Affairs at the time of the crisis and participated in the discussions in ExComm, made a surprising revelation in the 1992 Havana meeting:

that when officials in Washington examined the various proposals that
had originated in New York, they felt that Stevenson and McCloy were
anxious to reach a solution that would contribute to the prestige of the
UN, which is why they frequently told Stevenson and McCloy that
their proposals for negotiating with the Soviet Union were too weak
and should be strengthened; that they were making too many
concessions.

The draft protocol was discussed in a very tense atmosphere, the
same that surrounded all of the discussions that took place in the
course of the crisis. Its original version, with just a few paragraphs
modified, reflected the position of the three countries and mirrored
reality. This document has never been published and because of its
importance in the history of that dramatic period, I am including it in
full:

This protocol contains the agreement reached by the governments
of the Soviet Union, the Republic of Cuba and the United States,
as the result of an exchange of messages between N.S.
Khrushchev, Chairman of the Council of Ministers of the Soviet
Union, and John F. Kennedy, President of the United States; the
October 28, 1962, declaration by Fidel Castro, Prime Minister of
the Republic of Cuba; and the talks held by the representatives of
the above-mentioned governments with the participation of U
Thant, Secretary-General ad interim of the United Nations.

Chapter I. Article 1. The government of the United States
suspends all of the measures it took on October 24 of this year
with regard to ships going to the Republic of Cuba.

Article 2. The U.S. armed forces that were concentrated in the
southeastern part of the United States because of the measures the
United States took in the Caribbean area will be withdrawn as
quickly as possible.

Article 3. The government of the United States reaffirms the
October 27 declaration that John F. Kennedy, President of the
United States, made in his message to N. Khrushchev, Chairman
of the Council of Ministers of the Soviet Union, on the United
States' renunciation of an invasion of Cuba and the U.S.
government's confidence that other countries in the western
hemisphere would be willing to proceed in the same way. The
government of the United States will oppose those who seek to
carry out an attack against Cuba from U.S. territory. Likewise, the
government of the United States will keep the weapons of U.S.

origin that are sold or turned over to other Latin American governments from being used in an attack on Cuba.

Article 4. The United States will strictly respect the sovereignty of the Republic of Cuba and the inviolability of its borders, including its airspace and jurisdictional waters, and will not meddle in the internal affairs of the Republic of Cuba.

Article 5. The government of the United States declares that it will adopt all necessary measures and make the appropriate efforts to achieve the cessation, both in U.S. territory and in the territories of other countries in the western hemisphere, of all subversive activities against the Republic of Cuba, such as the dropping or launching of weapons and explosives by air and sea, the organization of invasions, and the infiltration of spies and saboteurs.

Article 6. The government of the United States will not hinder the Republic of Cuba's development of free trade and other economic relations with other countries.

Article 7. The government of the United States is willing to begin talks with the government of the Republic of Cuba on the evacuation of the Guantánamo Naval Base.

Chapter II. Article 8. The government of the Soviet Union declares that it has ended all work on installations designed for launching medium-range ballistic missiles with nuclear warheads in the territory of the Republic of Cuba, has dismantled those weapons and has returned them to the Soviet Union.

Article 9. The government of the Soviet Union, with the mutual agreement of the parties, has given the government of the United States the opportunity to verify that the Soviet party has fulfilled its obligations of withdrawing from Cuba the weapons mentioned in Article 8 of this protocol.

Chapter III. Article 10. The government of the Republic of Cuba declares its consent that the weapons mentioned in Article 8 of this protocol be dismantled and withdrawn from Cuban territory.

Article 11. The government of the Republic of Cuba reiterates that its foreign policy is based on strict compliance with the principles of the Charter of the United Nations, including that of noninterference in the internal affairs of other countries.

Chapter IV. Article 12. The contracting parties agree to accept the plan of U Thant, Secretary-General ad interim of the United Nations, on the presence of the United Nations in the Caribbean area by means of the establishment of observation posts for representatives of that organization in order to fulfill the purposes of this agreement. U Thant, Secretary-General ad interim of the United Nations, will work out the details of this plan in agreement with the contracting parties.

Article 13. It was agreed that on matters relating to the subsequent normalization of the situation regarding Cuba and other matters mentioned in the messages of N. Khrushchev, Chairman of the Council of Ministers of the Soviet Union, and John F. Kennedy, President of the United States, and in the October 28, 1962, declaration by Fidel Castro, Prime Minister of the Republic of Cuba, the talks between the interested parties would continue, in order to draw up mutually acceptable solutions.

Article 14. The parties agreed to present this protocol to the Security Council so it might take the corresponding measures, in conformity with the Statutes of the United Nations.[119]

This was the modified text. Most of the changes were unimportant. The more important ones were the elimination of an Article 9 under which the Soviet Union agreed that persons chosen from among the representatives of nonaligned countries and empowered by the Security Council should verify the withdrawal of the weapons from Cuba. An Article 10 was also eliminated, in which the Soviet Union reiterated its consent to the Secretary-General's proposal to give representatives of the International Red Cross access to the Soviet ships that were going to Cuba, so as to verify that they did not transport nuclear weapons. These were ideas that were put forward in the United Nations that never had much support – in the first case, because of Cuba's refusal, and, in the second case, because the Soviet Union said it didn't make sense, since it had already arrived at an agreement with the United States, and that was a prerequisite it didn't have to meet.

U Thant asked us to modify Article 12, saying that he wasn't the author of the plan for a multiple inspection in the Caribbean; several countries had suggested the formula, and he had adopted it to present it to the negotiators, but without claiming authorship. In that talk with Kuznetsov and me, U Thant warned that if the initiative weren't acceptable to all countries he would withdraw it; he stated that above all it should be acceptable to the Latin American countries.

The idea was that United Nations observers would go not only to Cuba but also to the United States – the Florida area – Puerto Rico

---

[119] Unofficial translation from the Spanish text.

and other places from which groups set out to attack Cuba, to inspect them and avoid new attacks on the island. Cuba expressed its agreement, since this meant verifications not only in its territory but also in that of other countries. The United States rejected the proposal, for it wouldn't allow UN observers in its territory.

Washington was aware that the protocol had been drawn up, and I suspect that if the question of multiple inspections had been presented formally at that time, the Latin American countries would have rejected it, thus pulling the chestnuts out of the fire for the United States, making it unnecessary to open its own mouth. The United States rejected the inspections in private talks; if the proposal had been made public, the Latin American countries which contained CIA bases for operations against Cuba would have also refused to allow any inspection.

U Thant rewrote Article 12 of the draft protocol to read as follows: "The contracting parties agree to accept the plan on the presence of the United Nations in the Caribbean area by means of the establishment of observation posts by representatives of that organization in order to fulfill the purposes of this agreement. The Secretary-General ad interim of the United Nations will work out the details of this plan in consultation with the interested parties."[120]

When we discussed U Thant's text, I observed to Kuznetsov that the statement would be stronger if it said that the idea was his, since, as mediator in the conflict by mandate of the Security Council, he had the most authority for getting the multiple inspection accepted. But Havana and Moscow accepted it as it was, keeping in mind what the Secretary-General had stated. The day after the protocol was completed, the Soviet negotiators presented it to McCloy and Stevenson for their consideration.

While these efforts were being made, the UN General Assembly met. As always, it had a very full agenda, which covered the important problems of the international community, but attention was concentrated on the exchanges that were going on between Havana, Moscow and Washington and on the role that the United Nations was playing in the controversy.

On November 15, a letter from the Prime Minister of Cuba addressed to the Secretary-General reached UN headquarters; in it, the Cuban leader called his attention to the significant increase in the number of incursions by warplanes over Cuban air bases, flying close to the ground over military defenses and taking photographs not only

---

[120] Translated from Spanish.

of the dismantled strategic missile installations but of all the island. He also reported the recent capture of the head of a group of spies trained by the Central Intelligence Agency, which had enabled the Cubans to learn how the photos obtained by the spy planes were used in directing sabotage — which, in that particular operation, was planned against an industry employing 400 people, who would have been killed if the plan hadn't been discovered.

Fidel Castro warned that those violations couldn't be permitted and that he shouldn't be asked to accept them in view of the discussions about the crisis that were taking place, and he informed the Secretary-General that any warplane that violated Cuba's sovereignty by invading its airspace could do so only at the risk of being destroyed if it came within range of Cuba's antiaircraft weaponry. As already stated, President Kennedy had announced over television on November 2 that his administration had confirmed the dismantling of Soviet missile bases, that the missiles and all their apparatus had been placed in crates and that the permanent installations in those places had been destroyed. What was the purpose, then, of the flights in those days? And the flights of the U-2s?

A brief review of the history of air incursions by the Pentagon, committed inside not only in other countries, but also the United States, would not be amiss. The first spy mission was carried out over the Soviet Union, in the Leningrad area, on July 4, 1956.[121] That same year, at the time of the crisis over the nationalization of the Suez Canal, U-2s took photographs of British, French and Israeli bases in Malta, Toulon, Cyprus and Israel without informing their governments.[122] The British were given aerial photographs of the Canal.[123] After the triumph of the revolution in Cuba in 1959, Eisenhower ordered aerial reconnaissance over the Zapata Peninsula, in the south-central part of Cuba, by U.S. Navy planes that were supposedly heading for the Guantánamo Naval Base.[124] The first U-2 flight over Cuba took place on October 27, 1960, on Eisenhower's instructions.[125] Washington also used U-2s to plan troop actions inside the United States itself. This was done in 1963 during the mass protests against racial segregation, both in the South and the North, when thousands of U.S. citizens were jailed and people were hurt in the clashes between demonstrators and the police and National Guard. On that occasion, Kennedy sent the same

---

[121] Brugioni, *Eyeball to Eyeball*, 30.

[122] Ibid., 33.

[123] Hugh Thomas, *Suez* (New York: Harper and Row, 1969), 70.

[124] Brugioni, *Eyeball to Eyeball*, 41.

[125] Ibid., 55.

planes that had flown over Cuba during the Missile Crisis to take pictures in the State of Alabama.[126]

Washington's acts of provocation created a state of alarm among diplomats at UN headquarters, who hoped that the crisis had ended. If the U.S. military planes continued their flights and some of them were shot down, the impact of the situation would monopolize the attention of the General Assembly. The prevailing view in the Assembly, apart from that of the United States' allies, was sympathetic toward Cuba's position in defense of its sovereignty, but it was also clear that everyone wanted the confrontation ended as quickly as possible.

In a letter that Kennedy sent to Khrushchev on November 15, which was made public in 1992, Kennedy mentioned a Brazilian proposal which was on the agenda of the General Assembly, about the denuclearization of Latin America. Kennedy said that it would be acceptable if Cuba and the other countries in the western hemisphere cooperated with it. Unquestionably, it would serve the interests of the United States, since it would take away other countries' rights to have the weapons they wanted, while the United States would retain and enlarge its nuclear arsenals.

On November 16, Cuba took up several topics in the General Assembly, including the Brazilian initiative. The draft resolution had been presented a week earlier. The initiative pledged that the Latin American countries would not manufacture, receive, store or test nuclear weapons or devices for their transportation; that they would get rid of any nuclear weapons and/or launching vehicles that might be in their territory; and that they would make arrangements for verifying these provisions, to show that, in fact, their pledges had been kept. It also called on all countries in the world to support this agreement, to make Latin America a denuclearized zone.

The discussion took place in the First Commission. I said that Cuba was in favor of general and complete disarmament but that it should be real disarmament, not just arms control. The role of protagonist that Cuba was playing in a situation caused by the U.S. government, which had pushed the world to the brink of thermonuclear war, gave Cuba the right to issue a call to all countries, asking them to exercise their influence to help reach an agreement that would fully satisfy humanity's longing for peace, since experience showed that walls would have to be built to stop the aggressors.

---

[126] William Manchester, *The Glory and the Dream* (New York: Bantam Books, 1985), 979 and 980.

Cuba understood that disarmament had to be closely linked to security. For example, I said that the continual blockade of a nation created the conditions for a conflagration. A policy of force, such as U.S. policy on Cuba, manufactured pretexts for aggression. I then pointed out that, even though many orators had spoken out for easing international tension, Washington was maintaining its illegal naval blockade of Cuba, continuing its aggressive flights over Cuban territory, stepping up its sabotage plans, engaging in even worse anti-Cuba propaganda, and trying to get third countries to divert ships with food and raw materials for Cuba's industries away from Cuban ports.

Cuba extended its goodwill to the Brazilian initiative, which unquestionably arose because of the negotiations that were being held, but I pointed out that it was necessary to include some precepts to round it out. First of all, the pledge not to manufacture, receive, store or test nuclear weapons, as set forth in the draft, wasn't enough to free the Latin American nations from the horrors of modern warfare. Latin America could cleanse its territory of those weapons and still be attacked by other powers. Therefore, the nuclear powers should give guarantees that they wouldn't use their weapons against that part of the world. Another important aspect that needed clarification was that, while Latin America would renounce the presence of those weapons of mass destruction, strategic points where one of the nuclear powers stored those weapons — such as Puerto Rico and the Panama Canal Zone — could not be exempted from the measure. And, lastly, it was absolutely necessary to close down all of the military bases in Latin America that belonged to nuclear powers, because there was no moral or logical reason why — to take the case of the U.S. base at Guantánamo, in Cuban territory — one of the nuclear powers should be allowed to have that base there while Cuba could not have a base belonging to a friendly country for its own defense. Brazil withdrew its proposal the next month, to be considered at another time.

Kuznetsov and McCloy met on November 18. The U.S. representative informed Kuznetsov that he hadn't been able to study the draft protocol because he had been in Washington to welcome Chancellor Adenauer of Germany. However, he said, the United States would not make any pledges in the form of a protocol, because they would be equivalent to a treaty and would have to be approved by Congress, which would surely refuse to do so. He suggested that the three parties should send independent declarations to the Security Council. Later, he insisted on on-site inspections and spoke of the withdrawal of the IL-28 bombers. During their talk, he several times mentioned Cuba's threat that it would shoot at the U.S. planes, and he said that the flights within range of Cuban artillery had been suspended the day before. From what McCloy said, Kuznetsov understood that from then on the U-2s would be the only U.S. planes to fly over Cuba, and that the U.S. authorities were studying another form of on-site verification.

The Soviet negotiator then spoke of the idea of multiple verification in the Caribbean, with which McCloy said he wasn't familiar. Kuznetsov said that the protocol was a good basis for solving the problem and that the situation was ripe for it. He added that the Soviet Union had already complied with the main aspects of the pledge but that the United States had not yet fulfilled any of them.

Some of the talks between the Soviet and U.S. negotiators took place in their diplomatic missions, but many were held at the Soviets' country house at Glen Cove, Long Island, and at McCloy's home in Stamford, Connecticut, far from the hurly-burly of the United Nations. All of the contacts between the Cuban and Soviet representatives took place at the diplomatic headquarters of the two countries. The meetings with U Thant were always at his office in the United Nations.

During the first few days of the negotiations, Kuznetsov, Stevenson and McCloy concentrated on solving the small incidents that arose between Soviet and U.S. ships while the former were taking the atomic weapons back to the Soviet Union. Later, Stevenson and McCloy once again raised the question of on-site inspections and vigorously demanded the withdrawal of the IL-28 light bombers. Most of those planes, which belonged to the Soviet government, had not been used by the Soviet Air Force since the first half of the 1950s, and U.S. specialists didn't consider them to constitute a strategic threat. U-2s had photographed the planes' coverings on the decks of Soviet ships since September 28, and they hadn't caused any concern. It was known that the Soviet Union had supplied IL-28s to Egypt and Indonesia and that they had a limited capability. After the discovery of the nuclear missiles, the White House thought the matter was taking on other meanings, but there was still some disagreement, and Kennedy himself hesitated at one point about whether or not to demand their withdrawal. Some of Kennedy's advisers thought that the United States' main purpose had already been achieved with the return of the missiles, but others said that Kennedy ought to make the most of the situation by demanding the withdrawal of the missiles and include the planes, and that was the view that prevailed.[127]

---

[127] Raymond Garthoff, *Reflections on the Cuban Missile Crisis* (Washington, D.C.: The Brookings Institution, 1989), note on page 104. Repeated at the Havana conference.

In fact, Cuba held the IL-28s ready to be used for mining its sea accesses, hitting enemy groupings with bombs and torpedoes and engaging in air-naval exploration — exclusively defensive actions, in case of an invasion.[128]

On November 3, Stevenson told Kuznetsov that the planes should be withdrawn as quickly as possible. On November 5, U Thant asked Kuznetsov if the Soviet Union was going to withdraw the IL-28s, because the U.S. negotiators were very firm in their demand. That same day, Robert Kennedy pressured the Soviet ambassador in Washington on the same question. On November 8 and 13, the talks between the Soviet negotiator and McCloy and Stevenson were on that subject only.

In the talks between Fidel Castro and Anastas Mikoyan, who was in Cuba from November 2 through 26, the IL-28s were discussed in full. Cuba was opposed to the withdrawal of those planes, because they were needed to defend the island against attack. Mikoyan gave his assurance that the planes were not included in the U.S. demands or in the pledges Khrushchev had made to Kennedy. "What if the U.S. authorities demand that the IL-28s be removed?" Fidel Castro asked. Mikoyan replied, "To hell with the imperialists!"[129] A few days later, the Deputy Premier of the Soviet Union was forced to tell his host that, sure enough, the United States had made that demand — and, later, to tell him Moscow had agreed to it.

Fidel Castro not only foresaw the demand regarding the planes but also warned Mikoyan that Washington would also ask that the Komar torpedo boats be withdrawn after the missiles had been returned to the Soviet Union. "I know the U.S. officials better than you do," Fidel Castro told his disbelieving visitor. [130]

On November 5, Khrushchev wrote to Kennedy expressing his concern over the list of weapons that the United States called offensive — the list that had been given to Mikoyan and Kuznetsov at the airport in New York after the main problem had been solved with the withdrawal of the missiles. The Soviet leader said that the new demand aggravated the relations between the two countries. The next day, Kennedy insisted that the IL-28s be withdrawn and announced that U.S. planes would continue to fly over Cuba.

After his talks with Mikoyan in Havana, Fidel Castro sent U Thant a letter on November 19 that stated:

---

[128] Tomás Diez Acosta, *La Operación Anadir* [Operation Anadyr] (Havana: Publication of the Military History Study Center, 1991), 152.

[129] Tripartite Conference, fifth session, January 11, 1992, 25, translated from Spanish.

[130] Alexander Alexeev, Tripartite Conference, first session, January 9, 1992, 82.

The government of the United States and the most reactionary of the U.S. press are trying to present the Cuban government as hindering and sabotaging the possibilities for a peaceful solution to the present crisis. To do so, they base themselves on two of our people's entirely legitimate decisions: first, not to accept a unilateral inspection of our soil, an inspection with which the government of the United States seeks to make decisions on matters which are nobody's business but ours; and, second, not to permit invasions of our airspace which are injurious to our security and offensive to our national honor.

Now the United States has made the IL-28 light bombers the crux of the problem. Those planes are owned by the Soviet government. They were brought to Cuba for our country's defense. Because of their slow speed and low flight ceiling, they are outdated, compared to modern means of antiaircraft defense. It is clear that the U.S. government's position on demanding the withdrawal of those planes is simply a pretext for maintaining tension, prolonging the crisis and upholding its policy of force. Even so, if the Soviet government should consider it beneficial to the negotiations and the solution of the crisis that those planes be withdrawn, the Cuban government would not place obstacles in the way of implementing that decision.

At the same time, high-ranking officials of the U.S. government have stated that U.S. military planes will continue to violate Cuban sovereignty and invade our airspace. If there should be any incidents while those arbitrary acts are being perpetrated against our country, the U.S. government would be entirely responsible.

We are willing to consider a broad solution that would end the existing tension once and for all. The time has come for knowing who does and who does not want peace. If, in spite of the calm attitude of the Soviet Union and Cuba's willingness to work for an honorable, stable peace, the government of the United States persists in its acts of force against our country, nobody should have any illusions about the inevitable result of that policy. The United States constantly threatens our country with war. It would be a war without glory or honor against a nation that will never give up.

The next day, Khrushchev informed Kennedy that the planes would be withdrawn, and the naval blockade was lifted on November 21.

As was true of other episodes in the crisis, the controversy over the bombers was cloaked in rhetoric that did not always reflect what was really going on. The public messages and letters between the Soviet and U.S. leaders were the visible expression of the negotiations on the crisis, while confidential communications presented another version.

Now we know from documents that Washington declassified in January 1992 that Khrushchev told Kennedy on November 12 he was willing to remove the planes from Cuba. He wrote:

> Your brother Robert Kennedy mentioned as one variant of solving the question of IL-28 aircraft that those planes should be piloted by Soviet fliers only. We agree to this. But we are also ready to go further — we will not insist on permanently keeping those planes in Cuba. We have our difficulties in this question.
>
> Therefore, we give a gentleman's word that we will remove the IL-28 planes with all the personnel and equipment related to those planes, although not now but later. We would like to do that some time later when we determine that the conditions are ripe to remove them. We will advise you of that.[131]

On the evening of that same day, Robert Kennedy delivered his brother's proposal to the Soviet ambassador in Washington: that the planes be withdrawn in 30 days and that, even though he preferred that the date be made public, it would be all right if Khrushchev had difficulties in doing so, for he trusted he would keep his word. That message reached Moscow the next day.

On November 14, Khrushchev wrote to Kennedy again, answering his message. He told him that the 30-day limit was agreed to but that, if difficulties arose, the planes would be withdrawn in two or three months. The next day, the U.S. President wrote saying that he was glad that a month was acceptable. He didn't extend the time limit.

It wasn't until November 20, the day after Fidel Castro had written U Thant, that Khrushchev announced his decision to withdraw the bombers. No one in Havana knew that the Soviet Union had decided on November 12 to go along with Washington. This correspondence, which has now been made public, shows how Kennedy kept forcing Khrushchev back into a tighter and tighter corner.

---

[131] *The Kennedy-Khrushchev-Castro Correspondence*, 31-2.

The demand that the Soviet Union withdraw the bombers became a point of friction that the United States used to hold back the solution of the crisis and keep tension from being eased. When the missiles were returned to the Soviet Union, everybody thought that the main problem had been solved, that there was no justification for prolonging the naval blockade or continuing the spy flights, but world public opinion was deceived. Washington wanted to obtain more advantages from the Soviet Union, harass Cuba, establish the legitimacy of the violation of Cuba's airspace and ensure that the solution of the crisis wouldn't curtail the aggressive policy it maintained against Cuba. That was its main objective. In that private correspondence, Kennedy didn't contradict Khrushchev's view that it would be a good thing to end the conflict as quickly as possible, but neither did he take any steps to end it. The threat of taking drastic measures against Cuba was still there behind everything he said.

After receiving the November 20 letter from the Kremlin which stated that the bombers would be withdrawn, Kennedy called a press conference to announce the news and the lifting of the naval blockade. He said that, since no inspections had been made in Cuba, the prerequisites for promising that Cuba would not be invaded had not been met, and he added that peace in the Caribbean was dependent on Cuba's not exporting the aggressive designs of communism. In other words, the United States' own aggressive policy would be continued, even though there weren't any strategic weapons left in Cuba and the old bombers were thousands of miles away, in Soviet hangars.

At 3:30 on the afternoon of that same day, November 20, the U.S. President met with his advisers and ordered the suspension of low-altitude flights over Cuba, saying that the U-2 flights would continue. Dean Rusk informed his negotiators in New York that Kennedy favored individual declarations by the Soviet Union and the United States in the Security Council and that, once those declarations were made, the United States would keep its promise not to invade Cuba — as long as Cuba behaved.

Cuba's reaction to Kennedy's declarations was made public on November 25. The most important parts of that reply were the following:

> The statements by the President of the United States contain the germs of an aggressive policy of acts of provocation against our country, which should be denounced... The position of force taken by the U.S. government is contrary to international legal norms. In addition to carrying out attacks on Cuba, which pushed

the world to the brink of war, it even refused to provide any guarantees that it would not once again violate the Charter of the United Nations and international law by invading the Republic of Cuba on the pretext that our country had not agreed to allow international inspections.

President Kennedy's claim is groundless, a mere pretext for not keeping his part of the pledge and for persisting in his policy of aggression against Cuba. Moreover, even if an inspection were permitted that would provide all of the guarantees which it might occur to the government of the United States to demand, peace in the Caribbean is made conditional on Cuba not being used "to export communist aggression." Thus, any effort that the Latin American people may make to try to free themselves of the imperialist yoke could serve as a pretext for the U.S. government to accuse Cuba, break the peace and attack our country. It would be difficult to conceive of weaker guarantees than these.

Another thing also shows the aggressive, arrogant nature of the U.S. government's policy. In his latest statement, President Kennedy tacitly reaffirmed the right of spy planes to fly over Cuba's territory and photograph it from one end to the other. This, too, constitutes a gross violation of international law.

The only effective guarantee for maintaining international legality and ensuring that legal norms are obeyed is for all nations to abide by the established norms. In this time of sharp confrontation between two concepts of society, the United States has assumed the right to break the international norms in effect and to establish new formulas to suit itself. We believe that when such a dangerous situation is created and a country decides all on its own how to apply law in its relations with other countries in the world, there is no alternative but to firmly oppose its pretensions... Cuba will have to defend itself. It reserves the right to obtain weapons of any kind for its defense and will take whatever steps it deems pertinent to strengthen its security in the face of that declared threat. This is why, after President Kennedy's statement, it can be said that though an armed conflict was avoided peace has not been achieved.

The government of the United States demands that the United Nations verify in our territory that the strategic weapons have been withdrawn. Cuba demands that the United Nations verify in the territory of the United States, Puerto Rico and other places where attacks are prepared against Cuba that those training camps for mercenaries, spies, saboteurs and terrorists — the centers where subversion is prepared — and the bases from which the pirate boats set forth to attack our coasts have been dismantled... Moreover, as part of the guarantees which Cuba demands, effective control measures should be established to prevent those acts from being repeated in the future.

If the United States and its accomplices in aggression against Cuba don't allow the United Nations to make such inspections in their territories, Cuba will not accept such an inspection in its territory, either. A broad, honorable agreement that is acceptable to all can be achieved only by means of reciprocal concessions and guarantees. If such an agreement is reached, Cuba will not need strategic weapons for its defense, the number of foreign technical-military personnel for training the members of our Armed Forces will be reduced to a minimum, and the conditions will be created for developing our relations with all the countries in this hemisphere.

We don't believe in mere promises of non-aggression; it will take deeds to convince us. Those deeds are outlined in our five points. We have little faith in President Kennedy's words — as little as the fear instilled in us by his veiled threats. [132]

The declaration was signed by the national leadership of the Integrated Revolutionary Organizations and the Cuban Council of Ministers.

---

[132] *Posición de Cuba ante la Crisis del Caribe*, 89-94.

8

No inspections

A nastas Mikoyan's visit to Havana was an interesting episode in that historic era. Mikoyan, an old-time Bolshevik who was long accustomed to the exercise of power, was influential with Khrushchev and had been the first high-ranking Soviet to visit Cuba after the triumph of the revolution. He also signed the first agreement between Cuba and the Soviet Union. He had excellent credentials for carrying out the responsibility assigned to him: to pacify the Cuban leaders, who were less than happy with the way Moscow had handled events. His wife died while he was in Cuba, but he considered that his first duty was to complete the negotiations he had been entrusted with, at a time that was critical for his country, the world, and Soviet-Cuban relations, which were at an all-time low. He decided not to go to Moscow for her burial but to remain in Cuba until his task was completed.

Pressured by Washington and anxious to end the crisis as quickly as possible, the Soviet government wanted to convince Cuba to accept inspections in its territory. It was one of Mikoyan's most thankless tasks, faced with Cuba's refusal to give in to a demand that would undermine the country's sovereignty — a demand that, moreover, had no justification at that time, when the launching pads for the missiles were already being destroyed and the missiles were being shipped back to their points of origin. Even so, Mikoyan tried various formulas to obtain approval for the inspections, but none were acceptable to the Cuban government, because all of them disguised Washington's real purpose. I imagine that the Kremlin's envoy felt rather uncomfortable about the position he was in, because, in his messages to Kennedy, Khrushchev had accepted inspections in Cuba, and Mikoyan was expected to achieve the impossible: to protect his chief's position and to get the Cubans to accept an action that they had refused right from the start. In spite of his persuasive powers, Mikoyan failed in this.

The Deputy Premier of the Soviet Union was in Cuba for more than 20 days, participating in talks with Fidel Castro, either alone or with the rest of Cuba's political leaders. The talks were difficult, but, even so, Fidel Castro saw him off at Havana's airport with an effusive embrace, in recognition of his good intentions and hard work. Mikoyan also failed to convince the Cubans that the decision to withdraw the missiles had been made without first consulting the Cuban government, because Khrushchev didn't have time to do so, in view of the imminence of a U.S. military invasion of Cuba.

The talks with Mikoyan went through several stages, from some initial chilliness to lively debates of the opinions expressed, and finally to acknowledgment by both parties, who maintained their positions, that, after all, it was an episode that shouldn't cause a break between the two countries. Both countries were faced with a common enemy that sought to crush the Cuban revolution and continue its ideological and military offensive to wipe out the Soviet Union and its influence in a large part of the world. Fidel Castro described the talks as very difficult. The differences had made the Cuban government and people bitter. The five guarantees that Cuba demanded to ensure that Kennedy would keep his promise not to invade Cuba were restated, as was Cuba's position of not accepting the violation of its airspace under any conditions or pretexts. Before leaving for New York en route to the Soviet Union, Mikoyan declared publicly that Cuba could count on the Soviet Union's full support.

While Mikoyan was in Havana, the talks continued in New York. The draft protocol quoted in Chapter 7 had been in Stevenson and McCloy's hands since the middle of the month (McCloy turned out to be the main U.S. contact with the Soviets), and work was going ahead on alternate drafts to be submitted to the Security Council.

Although the most dangerous part of the crisis had passed with the return of the atomic ballistic missiles to the Soviet Union, the United States kept up the tension with its demands that inspections be made in Cuba and that Cuba be stripped of the IL-28s. Alarming rumors from Washington reached the circles frequented by the New York negotiators and filled the hallways of the United Nations, rumors to the effect that a military action against Cuba hadn't been discarded, adding new elements of uncertainty to the existing situation. It was said that the most hard-line sectors of the Pentagon had not lost hope of launching a military offensive against Cuba and that pressures continued to be exerted on Kennedy, in spite of everything he had already achieved in his dealings with Khrushchev. The naval blockade continued and, even though there was little or no possibility of a serious incident between the ships of the two big powers, since nothing had happened in the most dangerous days of the crisis, it could not be entirely ruled out.

The most frequent comments were that the invasion plans had been based on the military potential Cuba had before September and, with the withdrawal of the nuclear missiles, the country had gone back to its previous defense capability. It was taken for granted that the Soviet Union would remove its bombers, which is precisely what happened in that period. There was no reliable basis for the speculations of an invasion attempt, but there was also no way of knowing the truth. Now, after confidential documents from that period have been made public, it can be seen that the highest-ranking military chiefs were motivated by intransigent aggressiveness. This is shown, for example, in the U.S. Navy and Air Force chiefs' reaction when they learned of Khrushchev's October 28 letter announcing that the missiles would be withdrawn — a reaction that unquestionably reflected the feeling of large sectors in the Pentagon and the right-wing in both the Republican and Democratic parties. Moreover, there is the secret memorandum of August 2, 1962, that was submitted to the Special Group of Operation Mongoose, which spoke of intervention in Cuba and pointed out that Cuba's military capability was oriented toward defense. It is clear that plans for aggression, preparations for it and funds being collected for it were based on that fact — that Cuba was ready to defend itself, not attack anybody — and on the weapons Cuba had (which determined which weapons the aggressor would use). In view of that situation, according to the rumors that reached New York in November, the Pentagon was clearly tempted to implement its offensive plans. The plans drawn up in the summer of 1962 were still viable in November.

Operation Mongoose was interrupted when the Missile Crisis began, but the assumptions underlying its plans remained in effect in U.S. strategy. The declassified document on this is badly mutilated with deletions, but, even so, it shows some interesting aspects of the war plans. The parts of the text that were blacked out concern the personnel, units and equipment that were being readied to carry out the action; the largest units that would be used in the initial attack; the level of mobilization required; and the effects the act of aggression might have on the international community and how to react to them. A curtain was also drawn over the time the U.S. planners estimated it would take to control strategic key points in Cuba.

According to that document, U.S. military reaction would be largely determined by the Cuban Armed Forces' determination to stand firm, the weapons the Cubans had and their skill in handling them at the time of the military intervention. It contemplated a strong initial resistance to the attack, followed by a staunch defense of key points in the country and finally a long guerrilla war.

The United States estimated that Cuba had around 50 MiG fighter planes, some of which had light bombs. The memorandum noted that those which survived the attack could be used to attack targets in Florida. The U.S. analysts also estimated that Cuba had 11 B-26s, and those which survived the attack could be sent against targets in the southeastern part of the United States. The memorandum warned that Cuba's capability for confronting an invasion would be improved in the future with an increase in the weapons the Soviet Union would send it and that it was therefore important to move quickly to overthrow the Cuban government.

The memorandum said that it was impossible to state exactly how long the U.S. troops would remain in Cuba, because that would depend on many factors, including the resistance put up and the time needed to establish a government — if the U.S. troops were victorious, of course. It then went on to say, "Following the establishment of essential military control of the island, a substantial U.S. military commitment may be required in Cuba for a significant period of time. Post assault tasks will include restoration of law and order and the conduct of counter-guerrilla operations."[133] The document continued by noting that, to achieve those objectives, a large number of Army forces with sea and air support were required and that, "thereafter, a lengthy period of providing military assistance is anticipated."[134]

That was the situation as the United States saw it in October 1962 — which once again became reality after Khrushchev's October 28 letter, as may be supposed from General LeMay's and Admiral Anderson's reactions in the White House when they learned of that letter. The speculations in New York were made more meaningful by the subsequent revelations of the plans that were being discussed in

---

[133] *Cuba Between the Superpowers, 1961-1963*, a conference of U.S., Cuban and Soviet policy makers and scholars, held in Antigua, West Indies, January 3-7, 1991. The National Security Archives, Washington, D.C., Tab. 3, 216.
[134] Ibid.

Washington, even though it would be very difficult for the United States to attack Cuba and provoke a war while the nuclear missiles were on the high seas being taken to Soviet ports, as Fidel Castro has commented — but nobody was sure of anything. The Cuban revolution had badly upset the imperialist dreams of some very key sectors in the United States.

After returning to New York from Havana, Mikoyan had a long meeting with the U.S. negotiators at the Soviet Mission on November 26. The first thing he told Stevenson and McCloy was that he had given them a copy of the draft protocol two weeks before and he had not yet received their reply. Washington turned it down. The Soviets already had the first version of a U.S. text in their hands — which U Thant had also seen, because Stevenson had given him a copy on November 20. The Secretary-General and Kuznetsov told the Cuban authorities about the document, and I gave them our reactions to it. Mikoyan insisted that the protocol was the better formula, for it set forth the positions of the three parties. But he said that if the United States dug in its heels and refused to accept it, the Soviet Union would agree to having each of the three countries submit a unilateral declaration to the Security Council.

Mikoyan observed that the U.S. draft couldn't serve as the basis for any agreement, since it mentioned parts of Khrushchev's and Kennedy's statements and made the U.S. guarantee not to invade Cuba conditional on Cuba not committing any actions that might endanger peace in the western hemisphere. Since this demand wasn't included in any of the messages exchanged between the leaders of the Soviet Union and the United States, there were no grounds for making it — which, therefore, annulled the guarantee that there wouldn't be any invasion. Moreover, the draft attempted to legitimize the spy flights over Cuba and, while referring to supposed subversive activities by Cuba, made no mention of the subversive activities that the United States was in fact carrying out.

When Stevenson gave U Thant the copy of the U.S. draft declaration, he must have informed him that the U.S. government did not accept the multiple-inspection formula that was mentioned in Article 12 of the draft protocol. U Thant had informed the U.S. negotiators about the details of the plan on November 12. This was to create a group of UN observers: eminent individuals from nonaligned countries who would make on-site verifications of whether any nuclear weapons remained in Cuba. (All of them had already been removed by that date, as the U.S. authorities had confirmed.) They would also carry out on-site investigations of the CIA training camps for Cuban counterrevolutionaries in the Caribbean, Central America and Florida. U Thant had told the U.S. negotiators that Cuba would accept that solution if the United States and the countries that supported its policy on Cuba would accept it, too.

Mikoyan asked Stevenson and McCloy why the United States didn't agree to the initiative; they replied that the problem was there were military installations in Florida. Mikoyan said that those installations wouldn't be inspected — only the counterrevolutionaries' camps — so their argument didn't hold water.

Later, Mikoyan defended the five points that the Prime Minister of Cuba had presented as guarantees that the non-invasion pledge would be kept and as a means of normalizing international relations in the Caribbean. In the declarations that the Soviet leader had made at the end of his nearly three weeks' stay in Cuba, he said, "The five points constitute a program for struggling for peace; they contain no threats to anybody; they are fair and humane demands. This is a great program for peace for Cuba and for the Caribbean area, but it cannot be implemented without a struggle. All the Cuban people are struggling for it, and the Soviet Union considers this program to be fair and supports it in all possible ways."

It should be emphasized that the five guarantees which Cuba enunciated were never used as the basis for negotiation between the United States and the Soviet Union. At all times, the basis of the pact was that contained in the White House's and Kremlin's October 27 and 28 letters on the withdrawal of the missiles and the promise not to invade — without any effective guarantees — to which the return of the bombers was later added as a final condition for the United States' lifting the naval blockade. Together with this was the deal for removing the Jupiter missiles from Turkey and Italy in exchange for the missiles that were in Cuba.

The same day as that talk between the Soviet Deputy Premier and the U.S. negotiators, I met with U Thant to reiterate Cuba's positions and comment in general on the situation. Mikoyan and Kuznetsov had a meeting with the Secretary-General, as well. On November 27, Mikoyan invited me to the Soviet Mission for lunch and told me he had asked McCloy and Stevenson to let Cuba participate in the negotiations and that, though they had not agreed to the idea — probably waiting for a decision from Washington — they had not been completely opposed to it, either. Recently, I learned from a document declassified in the United States — containing a report on that meeting between Mikoyan and the U.S. representatives by Harlan Cleveland, Assistant Secretary of State for International Organization Affairs — that had recommended to the State Department and to the President that the Russians should be told the United States would break off the talks if they insisted on including the Cuban delegates in the final rounds of the negotiations.

Mikoyan also spoke with McCloy and Stevenson about the normalization of the relations between the United States and Cuba and was given a reply similar to that given to the request that Cuba be included in their negotiations in New York.

On November 28, Mikoyan went to Washington to meet with Kennedy and Dean Rusk. U.S. Ambassador Llewellyn Thompson, Soviet Ambassador Anatoly Dobrynin, and Yuri Vinogradov, of the Soviet delegation in the UN General Assembly, also took part in the talks. Right from the beginning, it was clear that Kennedy wasn't interested in discussing Cuba: he repeated all of his previous statements about the crisis and repeated what his representatives in New York had told Mikoyan. He neither added anything new nor opened up any possibilities for approaching the question from another angle. Every time Mikoyan tried to direct the conversation toward Cuba, the President spoke of the situation in Laos, where the Soviet and U.S. leaders were at loggerheads. Another point discussed was the possibility of a non-aggression agreement between the Warsaw Pact and NATO countries.

Kennedy said it would be better if the Soviet Union stopped thinking it had the mission of lighting the torch of revolution all over the world — it would be better than signing 40 treaties. Mikoyan replied that the Soviet Union wasn't responsible for revolutions and that the Soviet Union had not brought about the Cuban revolution. The President said that he wasn't accusing the Soviet Union of having fomented the Cuban revolution. Mikoyan said that there would be revolutions, no matter what the United States and the Soviet Union did. He went on to defend the five guarantees that Fidel Castro demanded and criticized the United States' aspiration of legitimizing its violation of Cuba's airspace.

That same day, in New York, a draft resolution was presented in the Security Council recommending that the General Assembly name U Thant as Secretary-General of the United Nations. As U Thant had said in Havana, no other candidate was supported by all sides.

By the end of the difficult process of negotiations, U Thant's role had become a secondary, marginal one. During my visit to him in his office on November 26, I said it was very important for the United Nations not to lose control of the negotiations and for him, personally, to continue to be the mediator, with the authority given him by his post. It was evident that Washington was controlling the discussions. I also warned the Soviet negotiator about this. It was clear that, after the United States rejected the protocol, nearly all discussions between Khrushchev's and Kennedy's delegates on how to get the Security Council to end the crisis were held without consulting U Thant, who was informed after the fact about what had been agreed upon. The Soviets kept Cuba informed about the U.S.-Soviet discussions, and Cuba had a chance to express its opinion about the documents that the two others were drafting. Moscow and Havana exchanged views about the work that was being done.

When I met with U Thant on November 26, he told me that the United States was considering two procedures for reporting to the Security Council. Under the first, a representative of each of the three countries would make a statement to the plenary, and the Chairman would sum up what each had said, winding up the session. Under the other procedure, the declarations would be sent in written form, without any need for the Security Council to meet, and the three statements would be recorded in a dossier on the case, without any subsequent action.

Even before the U.S. negotiators were given a copy of the draft protocol they weren't eager for a discussion in the Security Council. The United States feared it might turn into a public debate with Cuba in the United Nations in which the U.S. acts of aggression against Cuba and all its violations of international law and of the UN Charter would be brought out. Representatives of the nonaligned countries — who had already expressed their opposition to the naval blockade, since it rode roughshod over freedom of navigation on the high seas — would also be there. It was inevitable that the failure to respect the sovereignty of a small country — by continually violating its airspace — would also be discussed. A controversy on those terms would have tremendous repercussions, no matter how strict a press blackout was imposed, and it might make some ripples in the General Assembly if its session hadn't ended.

The United States wasn't afraid of a critical resolution in the Security Council, because it had veto power and its allies had a majority of the votes. Even so, there was a possibility that the Security Council might try to find some kind of long-term solution, linking it to the solution of the nuclear crisis, for the acts of aggression against Cuba had caused the conflict, and that fact couldn't be easily covered up. Moreover, the Secretary-General (who would have to report on the results of his efforts at mediation, a task entrusted to him by the Security Council) had stated in Havana in his meeting with Fidel

Castro that the two aspects — the short-term solution and the normalization of international relations in the Caribbean area — were linked, and he would have to go on record about the need to consider both expressions of the crisis as the only way to achieve peace.

The need to end all subversive, aggressive actions against Cuba and the economic blockade would also be examined as essential to a long-term solution, because such actions and the blockade were upsetting international relations in the Caribbean. The United States wouldn't have any arguments with which to justify its ignoring of international law, just as it hadn't been able to offer any excuse for not accepting inspections in its territory or in the countries from which the terrorists set out in expeditions against Cuba. That territory was also where the CIA operated training camps in sabotage for groups that made raids against Cuba — all this while the United States was demanding that Cuba should open its doors to foreign inspectors. It would be embarrassing for the members of the U.S. delegation to try to explain to the representatives of the nonaligned countries, who had suggested the initiative of multiple inspections, why the United States had rejected that formula, while Cuba had accepted it.

After the IL-28 bombers were withdrawn, the United States had no other demands to make, and it wanted to end the crisis as quickly as possible. At the last minute, the Soviets went along with this, agreeing with Washington to send the Security Council a joint letter without having a public debate in the highest body of the United Nations.

At first, the three countries had drawn up independent texts. Later, in November and December 1962, several drafts of a single statement were prepared in New York, in consultation with Washington, Moscow and Havana. Still later, the Soviet Union and the United States coordinated their efforts in a single declaration signed jointly, and Cuba made a draft document of its own. Since all of these formulas were to be presented in a session of the Security Council, the participants also worked on a draft resolution at the same time so the Security Council could examine it. As may be recalled, the Security Council had shelved its consideration of the crisis on October 25.

On December 4, I gave the Secretary-General the draft of Cuba's unilateral declaration (the Soviet negotiators already had a copy) so he would be familiar with it and convey it to the United States. The idea at that time was that each of the parties would make a declaration of its own, and each of the three parties would comment on the declarations of the other two. It wasn't a matter of reaching a compromise endorsed by the three countries; rather, what was sought was general agreement not entailing any obligations. Of course, that was a very remote possibility, and, in its statements, Cuba wished again to put on record the only conditions which might solve the crisis once and for all. In general terms, Cuba's declaration was similar to the provisions of the protocol. Since it was a unilateral document, for which Cuba alone was responsible, the United States' argument for rejecting the protocol — because it was equivalent to a treaty — wasn't applicable.

The Cuban text took into account the messages that Kennedy and Khrushchev had exchanged; the pledges that the United States and the Soviet Union had made as a result of those messages and later negotiations; and Cuba's position on the crisis, as expressed in its basic statements, such as President Dorticós' address to the General Assembly, Prime Minister Fidel Castro's televised October 23 speech, his October 28 declaration containing the five points and the November 25 joint declaration by the Integrated Revolutionary Organizations and the Council of Ministers.

In his appearance on Cuban television the day after Kennedy's announcement establishing the naval blockade and revealing that the missiles had been discovered, the Cuban leader gave a detailed review of the United States' policy of hostility from the last century up to the crisis, the failure of all its attempts to destroy the revolution, and the people's determination to continue on their independent path, no matter what the cost. He also noted that the negotiations held with the participation of the UN Secretary-General hadn't led to an effective agreement that could permanently guarantee peace in the Caribbean and end the existing tensions. They hadn't produced agreements that were acceptable to Cuba, because the government of the United States, far from renouncing its policy of aggression and intervention, maintained the position of force it had assumed in flagrant violation of international law. He repeated the demand for guarantees to ensure that the United States would keep its promise not to invade Cuba and said that Cuba would not accept inspections in its territory or permit spy flights.

In its unilateral declaration, the government of the United States said that firm agreements had been reached with the Soviet Union by means of the October 27 and 28 letters between Khrushchev and Kennedy and referred to their terms, adding that, according to the Soviet Union, the missiles had been withdrawn and the bombers would be returned to the Soviet Union by December 20. The U.S. declaration stressed that the Soviet Union would not introduce any "offensive" weapons into Cuba in the future.

It said that no agreement had been reached concerning on-site inspections in Cuba but that a procedure had been drawn up for verifications on the high seas. For this reason, the naval blockade had been lifted on November 20 and "that it was not the intention of the United States to invade Cuba... provided Cuba itself commits no aggressive acts against any of the nations of the western hemisphere."[135]

The document went on to say that the United States would employ other methods of observation and verification until effective arrangements had been made for a necessary safeguard to ensure that such weapons systems would not be introduced into Cuba again. It wound up by stating, "Nothing herein contained in any way affects the rights and obligations of any treaty or existing agreement to which the United States of America or the Soviet Union is a party."[136] This last sentence was a modification of the original text, which had mentioned the Inter-American Treaty of Reciprocal Assistance. The Soviets hadn't accepted this, since it referred to a pact between the United States and the Latin American countries, which had nothing to do with the Soviet Union.

The draft declaration which the Soviet Union circulated said that because the government of the United States had lifted the naval blockade against ships going to Cuba and had declared that it would not invade Cuba or support any other invasion that originated in any country in the western hemisphere. The Soviet declaration also stated that all of the weapons were being dismantled and withdrawn from the territory of Cuba as part of an agreement between the government of the Soviet Union and the government of the United States, with the consent of the government of the Republic of Cuba. These weapons either had already been withdrawn from the territory of Cuba and sent back to the Soviet Union or would be withdrawn and sent back no later than December 20, 1962.

It further stated that the Soviet Union would not send such weapons to the territory of the Republic of Cuba in the future.

Moreover, it said that the government of the Soviet Union understood that the talks between the interested parties would continue in order to reach mutually acceptable solutions on the normalization of the situation in the Caribbean region.

Before outlining the other drafts and the observations made by Cuba, I should note here, respecting chronological order, that Khrushchev sent Kennedy a letter on December 10 saying that they had

---

[135] Proposed statement by the United States and the Soviet Union to be presented to the UN Secretary-General, December 12, 1962, 2. From the author's files.
[136] Ibid., 2.

reached the final stage of ending the tension surrounding Cuba. Relations between the United States and the Soviet Union were now taking a normal course, "since all those [missiles] placed by us on Cuban territory which you considered offensive are withdrawn... More resolute steps should be taken now to move towards finalizing the elimination of this tension. On your part you should clearly confirm at the UN — as you did at your press conference and in your messages to me — the pledge of non-invasion of Cuba by the United States and your allies."[137]

Later on in the letter, Khrushchev returned to this theme:

We believe that the guarantees for non-invasion of Cuba given by you will be maintained and not only in the period of your stay in the White House. That, to use an expression, goes without saying. We believe that you will be able to receive a mandate at the next election, too — that is, that you will be the U.S. President for six years, which would appeal to us. In our time, six years in world politics is a long period of time and during that period we could create good conditions for peaceful coexistence on earth and this would be highly appreciated by the peoples of our countries as well as by all other peoples.

Therefore, Mr. President, I would like to express a wish that you correctly appraise the situation. It is of special importance to provide for the exchange of opinion through confidential channels which you and I have set up and which we use. But the confidential nature of our personal relations will depend on whether you fulfill — as we did — the commitments taken by you and give instructions to your representatives in New York to formalize these commitments in appropriate documents. This is needed in order that all the peoples be sure that the tension in the Caribbean is a matter of the past and that normal conditions have now been really created in the world. And for this it is necessary to fix the assumed commitments in the documents of both sides and register them with the United Nations.[138]

Clearly, Khrushchev was already beginning to have doubts about how serious the U.S. government was in its promise not to attack Cuba, and the reply he received from the White House must have made him even less confident. No one in Cuba knew of this exchange, for the

---

[137] *The Kennedy-Khrushchev-Castro Correspondence*, 65-6.
[138] Ibid., 69.

correspondence was confidential and wasn't made public until 1992. If it had been known then, when the negotiations were going on in New York, our doubts about the validity of a promise that had absolutely no guarantees would have increased. Note Kennedy's evasiveness in replying to Khrushchev's request that the United States declare in the United Nations that it wouldn't invade Cuba:

> You refer to the importance of my statements on an invasion of Cuba and of our intention to fulfill them, so that no doubts are sown from the very start. I have already stated my position publicly in my press conference of November 20, and I am glad that this statement appears to have your understanding; we have never wanted to be driven by the acts of others into war in Cuba. The other side of the coin, however, is that we need to have adequate assurances that all offensive weapons are removed from Cuba and are not reintroduced, and that Cuba itself commits no aggressive acts against any of the nations of the western hemisphere. As I understand you, you feel confident that Cuba will not in fact engage in such aggressive acts, and of course I already have your own assurance about the offensive weapons. So I myself should suppose that you could accept our position — but it is probably better to leave final discussions of these matters to our representatives in New York. I quite agree with you that the larger part of the crisis has now been ended and we should not permit others to stand in the way of promptly settling the rest without further acrimony.[139]

Kennedy arrogantly ignored Khrushchev's request that he formalize his pledge in the United Nations. Simply, he made no mention of it and referred the matter to the negotiators in New York, who were already working to keep it from going to the Security Council, so the United States wouldn't have to assume any obligations in that high-level body of the international organization. That was very significant.

After the unilateral declarations were discarded, the Soviet Union and the United States submitted a joint declaration to consultation on December 12. That declaration repeated in general terms what the two countries had set forth in their unilateral statements. The Soviet Union mentioned the number of missiles that had been withdrawn (42) and the number of bombers (also 42), and said that representatives of the two countries had cooperated in the verifications on the high seas. It

---

[139] Ibid., 74-5.

also said that it would not again introduce weapons in Cuba that could be used for offensive purposes. The United States insisted that all means of observation should be used in the future, since it hadn't been possible to make on-site inspections. The Soviet Union, feeling that it had complied with the spirit of the messages between the two heads of government, felt that no observations or verifications were needed or justifiable in the future. But, the document continued, the United States didn't support this view.

In its observations, Cuba opposed the U.S. authorities' intention of continuing aerial espionage and the ambiguity of the U.S. promise not to invade. Moreover, Cuba never said that weapons which could be used for offensive purposes would not again be introduced into Cuba, because such a general statement could also refer to conventional weapons, if the United States felt like calling them offensive. Moreover, that reference didn't appear in any of the messages between Khrushchev and Kennedy. The joint declaration was also discarded.

In their unilateral draft declaration, the Soviets said that the weapons had been dismantled and withdrawn "with the consent of the Republic of Cuba." The Prime Minister of Cuba commented on this aspect in the 1992 Havana conference, setting forth the Cuban government's reasoning at that time:

> We were sure that they would take them [the missiles] away as they had brought them and no other possibility existed. We didn't try to prevent this or to raise obstacles to it, because, if we had opposed the missiles' departure, an absurd situation would have been created. We would have had to enter into conflict with the Soviets — our friends, our comrades, our brothers — with military officers who had stood beside us, ready to give their lives for us. I saw many Soviets cry on October 28, Soviet military chiefs crying over the news that the missiles would be withdrawn... All of them were upset, and what could we do? Try to use force? Were we going to use violence against the Soviets? If we had said, "No, the missiles aren't going to leave here," it would have been utterly crazy. We had no alternative, moral or political, to accepting the situation. We had to let the missiles be taken away, because anything else would have been senseless. Moreover, what good would they have been to us? We weren't familiar with them and didn't know how to operate them.[140]

---

[140] Fidel Castro, Tripartite Conference, fifth session, January 11, 1992, 23. Translated from Spanish.

When the Cuban people learned that the missiles were going to be shipped back to the Soviet Union, there was a kind of anticlimax to the tense situation that had begun a few months earlier. In the cities and rural areas of Cuba, in the armed forces and in the militia, in factories and universities and in all homes, disillusionment and frustration over losing those weapons which were to have defended the country against threats and uncertainties — losing them without gaining any advantages in compensation — created a state of depression. This exacerbated the indignation that was felt over Cuba not even having been contacted when the decision was made to withdraw the missiles and aircraft.

In New York, after the various draft declarations had been discarded, the draft resolution that had been drawn up to be submitted to the Security Council was revived, practically out of nostalgia, though it was already almost axiomatic that no sessions would be held. It was a document that could have been very important, but it was soon consigned to the diplomats' files. It read as follows:

1. The Security Council greets with satisfaction and expresses its approval of the agreement reached by the governments of the Soviet Union, the United States and the Republic of Cuba with the participation of Secretary-General ad interim U Thant on the measures for normalizing the situation in the southern part of the Caribbean, measures which will contribute to easing the tension that has arisen in the relations between countries.
2. The Security Council takes cognizance of the pledges that the governments of the Soviet Union, the United States and the Republic of Cuba have made in the declarations in the Security Council, to wit: (the texts of the three declarations follow).
3. The Security Council expresses its confidence that the governments of the Soviet Union, the United States and the Republic of Cuba will abide strictly by the pledges they have made and will help to consolidate trust between countries and universal peace.[141]

All hopes for a fair conclusion to the dangerous and dramatic conflict were buried in the interests of the prevailing politics of the Cold War.

On December 19, after receiving a message from Havana, I met with U Thant. By that time, there was no doubt that many people wanted to avoid a debate in the Security Council, blocking the path for

---

[141] UN document. Author's file.

later peace efforts in the Caribbean and for any rectification of the U.S. policy of aggression. The point on Cuba remained on the Security Council's agenda, and was destined to become yet another of the many bundles of papers filed away in the UN offices. In reality, international interest had fallen off sharply following the Soviet-U.S. understanding on the weapons in Cuba, but the Secretary-General, who continued to act as mediator, could have taken action to revive the negotiating process before the chance to do anything was lost.

I asked U Thant if, in the covering letter he was going to send to the President of the Security Council accompanying the declarations of Cuba, the United States and the Soviet Union, he would include an appeal to the members of the Security Council and to all the other members of the organization – if he considered this feasible – asking them to continue examining the crisis in the Caribbean. Only a first session had been held, and more efforts should be made to achieve a definitive solution of the situation that had caused the dangerous confrontation.

U Thant didn't send any letter. Perhaps he thought that a few lines appended to his acknowledgment of receipt of the declarations that the countries sent him would be sufficient, but of course, it wasn't the same. In those lines, the Secretary-General expressed his confidence that, "all governments concerned will refrain from any action which might aggravate the situation in the Caribbean in any way."[142] It isn't hard to imagine what effect that advice had on the White House, the Pentagon and the CIA's offices in Langley.

How was the crisis formally ended? With two letters to U Thant: a very short one signed by Adlai Stevenson and V. Kuznetsov, jointly, and a very long one I signed on behalf of the Cuban government. Both were dated January 7, 1963.

The Soviet-U.S. letter reads:

On behalf of the governments of the Soviet Union and the United States of America we desire to express to you our appreciation for your efforts in assisting our governments to avert the serious threat to peace which recently arose in the Caribbean area.

While it has not been possible for our governments to resolve all the problems that have arisen in connection with this affair, they believe that, in view of the degree of understanding reached between them on the settlement of the crisis and the extent of progress in the implementation of this understanding, it is not

---

[142] U Thant, *View from the United Nations*, 194.

necessary for this item to further occupy the attention of the Security Council at this time.

The governments of the Soviet Union and the United States of America express the hope that the actions taken to avert the threat of war in connection with this crisis will lead toward the adjustment of other differences between them and the general easing of tensions that could cause a further threat of war.[143]

The Cuban letter reads:

On the instructions of my government I have the honor to send to you, with the request that they be forwarded to the President of the Security Council, copies of the letter which Fidel Castro, Prime Minister of the Revolutionary Government of Cuba, sent to you on October 28, 1962, and of the statement issued November 25, 1962, by the National Directorate of the Integrated Revolutionary Organizations and the Council of Ministers, so that they may be included in the Security Council's documentation on the Caribbean crisis.

At the same time I should be grateful if you would request the President of the Security Council to give instructions for these documents to be circulated to member states and if you would also arrange for the text of this letter to be circulated to all member states of the United Nations.

As you know, the negotiations initiated with your generous assistance have not led to an effective agreement capable of guaranteeing permanent peace in the Caribbean and eliminating the existing tensions.

The Revolutionary Government of Cuba considers that the basic reason why these negotiations have not led to agreements acceptable to Cuba is that the government of the United States, far from having renounced its aggressive and interventionist policy towards the Republic of Cuba, has maintained the position based on force which it took up in flagrant violation of the rules of international law.

The Cuban government has stated — and it wishes to reiterate it on this occasion — that it cannot regard any agreement as effective unless it takes into consideration the five points put forward as minimum guarantees for peace in the Caribbean.

---

[143] UN document. Author's file.

These measures were outlined by our Prime Minister, Fidel Castro, in his statement of October 28, 1962, which is attached.

These Cuban requests are based on elementary principles of international law. They are not irrational demands, and Cuba considers that no one in the United Nations could validly object to them without disregarding the very foundations of the world organization. The Cuban government therefore considers that the U.S. government's mere promise not to invade Cuba, which, moreover, has never been given formal shape, would not be any safeguard for our country and would not guarantee peace in the Caribbean.

We wish to draw attention to the fact that the U.S. government refuses even to give an assurance that it will not again violate the UN Charter by invading the Republic of Cuba. This is apart from the acts of aggression it has committed against Cuba and its preparations to carry out an armed invasion of our country — which brought the world to the brink of war, an outcome avoided by means of agreements which presupposed a commitment by the United States to abandon its aggressive and criminal policy towards Cuba. The United States refuses to give this assurance on the pretext that our country has not agreed to international inspection, as has been publicly stated repeatedly throughout this whole affair.

The Cuban government considers that it is a sovereign right of the nation concerned to agree or not to agree to inspection of its territory and that it is an absurd piece of insolence to offer an undertaking not to invade — the equivalent of an undertaking not to commit an international crime — upon the condition that the country liable to invasion agrees to inspection of its territory.

The government of Cuba considers, on the other hand, that the Soviet government has fulfilled the conditions concerning verification proposed by Chairman Nikita Khrushchev in his letter of October 28, 1962, by allowing the withdrawal of intermediate-range ballistic missiles with nuclear warheads to be verified on the high seas and by agreeing to similar methods of verification with regard to IL-28 bombers. Thus the U.S. government's claim has no foundation or practical purpose and is merely an excuse for it not to carry out its part of the agreement and to persist in its policy of aggression against Cuba.

The government of Cuba, moreover, categorically rejects the statement by the U.S. government in which it reserves the right to use other means of inspection and verification on its own account.

For a power to officially announce its decision to inspect the territory of another member state is truly alarming and amounts to a challenge to the United Nations. It implies an intolerable violation of national sovereignty, which Cuba denounces.

The Revolutionary Government of Cuba has already said that it would be ready to agree to the establishment of a system of multiple verification in the countries of the Caribbean region, including the corresponding parts of the United States, under which the extent of each countries' compliance with their undertakings could be verified. This is providing that the United States, for its part, would agree to the adoption of the five measures or points requested by the Cuban government.

The Cuban government regrets the fact that the negotiations carried out with the agreement of the Security Council, which you yourself nobly and impartially set in motion, have not led to a satisfactory conclusion capable of guaranteeing peace in this hemisphere and thus throughout the world.

The recent history of this crisis, we repeat, gives palpable proof that the responsibility for this failure and for maintaining the tensions which dramatically and recently aroused the fears of all humanity lies exclusively with the government of the United States.

The Revolutionary Government of Cuba wishes to state once more on this occasion that there is no better procedure for solving crises such as this than peaceful negotiations and discussion between the governments concerned, respecting the sovereign rights of each nation and the rules of international law which govern the coexistence of nations. This is not the criterion which has determined the behavior of the U.S. government, and its stubborn resistance to any lasting, satisfactory and fitting settlement is the reason why we are today unable to hail a real solution to the crisis.

Cuba reaffirms its peaceful policy and its desire for peaceful solutions, but wishes to state once more, in the words of the attached statement by the National Directorate of the Integrated Revolutionary Organizations and the Council of Ministers, that "to their positions of strength we shall answer with our firmness; to the intent to humiliate us, our dignity; to aggression, the resolve to fight to the last person."

The Cuban people, as our Prime Minister said during the recent ceremonies commemorating the fourth anniversary of the [1959] revolution, "reserve in full the right when confronted by their imperialist enemies and imperialist aggressors always to take any measures and to possess any weapons they consider appropriate."

We have not renounced this right.

Accept, sir, the assurances of my highest consideration.

Carlos M. Lechuga

Ambassador

Representative of Cuba to the United Nations[144]

Both the Soviet and U.S. negotiators thought of giving separate press conferences on January 7, but they called them off at the last minute, almost certainly to avoid difficult questions.

I have already noted that, in the final stage of the negotiations, U Thant had been somewhat pushed aside, especially by the U.S. representatives. That fact, obvious at the time, was confirmed in a document that the State Department declassified in February 1991. It reported on information that McCloy gave about his talks with Mikoyan on the points they were going to raise in the Security Council. The document referred to the Secretary-General and the efforts he had made throughout the crisis; the Soviets wanted to put that on record, and McCloy said that the United States wouldn't be inflexible about mentioning U Thant, but that no other concessions would be made. That is, it was a concession to include the name of U Thant in the declaration they were drawing up.

The same document, a part of which is still deleted, states that McCloy made some suggestions to Kennedy for use in his meeting with Mikoyan in the White House. One was that Kennedy should tell the Deputy Premier of the Soviet Union that, if the Soviet Union still intended to include the Cubans in the discussion of the final arrangements, the United States would examine the alternative of unilaterally breaking off the negotiations.

At one point, Kuznetsov told me of the possibility that I might take part in the discussions with Washington's representatives, but the idea was never considered formally, and the Soviet negotiator never mentioned it again — almost certainly because he already knew how intransigent the U.S. government was about this. Having Cubans take part in the discussions would make it more difficult for the United States to maintain its policy of aggression against Cuba, because the Cubans would obviously suggest solutions and the adoption of pledges aimed at stabilizing the situation in the Caribbean, ending tensions and

---

[144] UN document. Author's file.

halting acts of aggression. Note that Washington was considering breaking off the negotiations at the end of a difficult, anguishing process, which would mean abandoning the pledges it had made to Moscow in spite of whatever effect that might have on world and U.S. public opinion. It would have been interesting to see if it was really ready to take that political risk. Far from being extraneous to the conflict, Cuba was one of its main protagonists.

As soon as the letters were sent to U Thant for him to pass on to the President of the Security Council, the United States resumed its plans of subversion against Cuba. There was no transition period between the formal ending of the crisis and the revival of plans for aggression. At the same time, a period of détente between the two big powers began, accompanied by the stepping up of the arms race. Some surprising changes came about in the following year, 1963. Kennedy had only a few months left to live.

9

Aggression and détente

U Thant passed on the letters from the three countries, ending the process of negotiation, to the President of the Security Council on January 7, 1963. The next day, an announcement was made in Washington that an Interdepartmental Group had been formed to coordinate plans on Cuba. It goes without saying that those plans were of a subversive nature. Sterling J. Cottrell, Assistant Secretary of State for Inter-American Affairs, headed the Group. He was just the man for the job: his record showed that he was an expert in clandestine work, especially in guerrilla warfare in Vietnam and Laos, countries where the United States had already intervened in a major way. The Pentagon and the Central Intelligence Agency were among the government agencies represented in the Group, which clearly showed that diplomacy wasn't going to be its strong suit.

The first report that Cottrell made to McGeorge Bundy, the President's Special Assistant for National Security, stated that the Defense Department still favored "increasing degrees of political, economic, psychological and military pressures."[145] There were no doubts about the United States' intentions and the wide range of measures it was considering to achieve its objective.

A few days before the Interdepartmental Group was created, ExComm (the Executive Committee of the National Security Council) had been reestablished as the Standing Group, responsible for formulating policy on Cuba. It had only five members: Robert

---

145 Schlesinger, *Robert Kennedy*, 580.

Kennedy, John McCone, Robert McNamara, McGeorge Bundy and Theodore Sorensen.[146] The closely-woven network of bureaucratic teams that were to examine the options on Cuba included a special group headed by Bundy, which approved clandestine actions.

As the official archives of the United States have gradually been made public, some interesting aspects of that policy have been revealed. Sometimes they are contradictory, but the aggressive nature of the measures that were proposed and the actions that were carried out always prevailed over any other aspect. They showed the existence of a silent struggle within the U.S. government on what path to follow in the days after the Missile Crisis. The same thing happened regarding the United States' relations with the Soviet Union — although, in that case, the proposals for a policy of détente occupied an important place. That was not so with Cuba, the third side of the triangle within which the hurricane winds of confrontation were blowing; tensions were never eased in U.S.-Cuban relations. Just as Cuba had been excluded from the final negotiations on the crisis, so it was left out of the new stage that began between the two big powers in the international arena. Cuba had no rest or respite; the United States kept right on hammering away.

As evidence of the different nuances that were expressed in Washington's analysis of the Cuban problem, Bundy gave Kennedy a memorandum on January 4, 1963, that set forth the idea of exploring a rapprochement with Fidel Castro. On April 24, according to the declassified documents, Bundy stated in the Standing Group that the U.S. government's policy on Cuba should be based on reaching an agreement with the Cuban government, to keep Cuba from establishing a military force that might serve as an instrument for effecting revolutionary changes in Latin America. At the same time, the United States would work with its allies to isolate the Havana regime, counter Cuba's influence in Latin America by promoting socioeconomic programs and pursue a line of not engaging in a military invasion.

Those initiatives showed that the United States was at a crossroads and had no clear idea of which path to take. The internal conflict was between one sector that was determined to continue the boundless hostility and another that thought it might be possible to achieve the same goals though some kind of understanding with the Cuban government. Was coexistence with the Cuban revolution on the basis of sovereign equality between the two countries ever considered,

---

[146] Ibid.

or did the United States want to neutralize the revolution, offering
Cuba benefits if it abandoned its principles? That question has never
been answered. Cuba always wanted negotiations on the basis of
equality, in which we could discuss all of our differences without
infringing on our country's free will, independence and sovereignty,
but the United States has never been amenable to that.

The feelers that Kennedy put out in late 1963 to normalize
relations between the two countries showed the extent of those
differences. His intentions have remained an enigma, because he was
assassinated in Dallas before he could take any further steps.

After the negotiations that ended the crisis, the United States and
the Soviet Union began to experiment with new kinds of relations that
allowed them to continue their international ideological dispute
without falling into such a dangerous confrontation as the one they had
in October. The tensions between them were eased in some aspects, yet
not so much as to end the Cold War: paradoxically, the arms race was
stepped up tremendously in the ensuing years, involving an enormous
expenditure of resources, while, at the same time, the dialogue
continued with less strain. The frictions in Berlin and Laos that had
held the attention of the two governments in previous years gradually
dropped out of their discussions. The Soviet Union, which had felt the
weight of its adversary's nuclear superiority, was engaged in quickly
increasing its arsenal of atomic and conventional weapons and the
United States also increased its own, so as not to lose the advantage it
had gained. Both of them made technological advances, making the
means of mass destruction at their disposal even more lethal. That
development of military capability to achieve parity or maintain
superiority didn't clear the international atmosphere but became a new
factor of destabilization. The number of strategic and tactical nuclear
weapons and carrier systems grew from thousands in 1962 to tens of
thousands, both in their own territory and in their submarines. Though
not directly related to Cuba, that competition became more acute as a
result of the Cuban crisis.

Neither détente, which had some expressions in 1963, or the arms
race or the few agreements that were reached — limiting some
weapons that made no serious dent on the core of the competition —
detracted from the ideological struggle. The scene was always set by
fundamentally different concepts of society and socioeconomic
systems, the moral principles they defended and the project of social
justice that one wanted to achieve — while the other sought to freeze
the status quo.

Before and after the crisis, the ideological factor prevailed in the clashes between Cuba and the United States, and this, together with the United States' determination to exercise hegemony over the island, colored the period. The United States' policy against Cuba was exactly the same before and after the missiles; the resolution of the crisis didn't change anything. The rhetoric employed by the U.S. President and members of Congress, echoed by the press, never let up. The covert actions and conspiracies for assassinating the head of the Cuban revolution continued, as well.

In February 1963, the U.S. Joint Chiefs of Staff were asked to make an extensive study on actions to be taken in case of an uprising in Cuba, with a view to action in the following contingencies:

- a possible military and paramilitary response by the United States in case of a rebellion;
- how to ensure that the rebels received weapons and equipment;
- under what circumstances intervention should be considered; and
- whether or not to quickly implement OPLAN 316 (the invasion plan of the Atlantic Command, CINCLANT) in order to exploit the effects of an uprising among Castro's forces, if the revolt was extended and seemed to be successful.

The Joint Chiefs of Staff sent the petition on to CINCLANT, which responded on February 26, recommending that planes and submarines be used to supply the supposed rebels secretly with weapons and equipment until their military potential was developed enough to justify overt military action by the United States. The subversive plans which were being implemented were aimed at causing a situation which would lead to a military attack.

Washington approved a program of sabotaging electric power plants, oil refineries and sugar mills, to be implemented between November 1963 and January 1964. The House Sub-Committee on Inter-American Affairs undertook an investigation of Cuba's supposed subversive activities in the western hemisphere, and the Organization of American States passed a resolution for monitoring the trips that Latin Americans made to Cuba and for keeping an eye on the socialist countries' business transactions with Cuba. In March 1963, President Kennedy went to Central America and met with the presidents of those countries. They issued a declaration against Cuba. Warships and planes continued to circle the island as if the international situation hadn't changed since the end of the crisis. All those activities kept the Caribbean in a state of extreme tension. On the geopolitical map of the Pentagon, the CIA, the State Department and the White House, Cuba was still tied to the United States, which wouldn't let it go.

In March 1963, Cuban Foreign Minister Raúl Roa reminded the UN Secretary-General about the letter which was sent to him on January 7, 1963, at the end of the negotiations on the crisis. The Cuban letter said that the negotiations had not produced acceptable agreements, because the U.S. government hadn't renounced its policy of intervention against Cuba. As proof of this, Roa cited a long series of aggressive acts and statements, examples of which include:

- On January 8, 1963, it was revealed in Washington that the U.S. delegation to the United Nations had instructions to resort to all means to obstruct implementation of the UN Special Fund's project (which had already been approved) for a key agricultural experimental station in Cuba.
- In a televised interview on January 10, Edwin M. Martin, Assistant Secretary of State for Inter-American Affairs, made it clear that, in the strategy of aggression, Assistant Secretary Cottrell was going to coordinate Washington's policy on Cuba and serve as liaison with the Cuban community in exile. A few hours later, Cottrell named Lieutenant Colonel John Crimmings as its liaison with the counterrevolutionaries living in Miami.
- When Secretary of State Dean Rusk appeared before the Senate Foreign Relations Committee and the Foreign Affairs Committee of the House of Representatives, he said that the Kennedy administration had never promised not to invade Cuba.
- Senator Barry Goldwater told the press in Syracuse, New York, that he was suggesting that the naval blockade of Cuba be reestablished and that groups be trained for engaging in sabotage.
- John Stennis, Chairman of the Senate Armed Services and Appropriations Committee, said that the United States should act even if all of the offensive weapons had been withdrawn from Cuba.
- Newspaper accounts on February 7 stated that the U.S. Army was planning to create a new group of counter-insurgency experts, based in the Panama Canal Zone, to help the Latin American governments tackle any revolts fomented from Cuba. Some days earlier, the Secretary of Defense had said that the Cubans didn't have ships for transporting tanks or any other important kind of

military materiel in the Caribbean Sea or anywhere else in Latin America.

- On January 10, Senator Hubert Humphrey stated that the United States wouldn't rest until Cuba — which he described as a focus of communist penetration — had been wiped out.
- New York Governor Nelson Rockefeller said he was disturbed by the situation in Cuba because it hurt private capital investments in Latin America.
- On February 11, a launch crewed by CIA agents was captured on the northern coast of Camagüey Province, in Cuba.
- On February 13, another CIA launch machine-gunned two small, unarmed Cuban fishing boats; two of the Cubans were wounded, and all of them were left on an uninhabited cay.[147]

Roa's denunciation also mentioned several other examples and warned about the wave of hysteria that was being fomented to pave the way for a full-scale attack. A few days later, a vessel manned by Cuban counterrevolutionaries — as announced in Miami — fired on and sank the Soviet merchant vessel *Baku*, which was loading sugar in the port of Caibarién, on the northern coast of Cuba. Earlier, another Soviet ship, the *Lvov*, had been attacked. Cuba and the Soviet Union protested to the United States about the attacks, and the White House, State Department and Justice Department declared that they neither supported nor approved of those actions carried out by Cuban "émigrés." However, General Victor Krulak, a counterinsurgency specialist working for the Joint Chiefs of Staff, in confidence told Captain Bradley Earl Ayers, a paratrooper who worked for the CIA, that the CIA had staged the operations. General Krulak said that the operations attributed to the exiles had been "planned and conducted under the supervision of the CIA... from bases in southern Florida."[148]

Even though the Missile Crisis had officially ended with the sending of letters to the President of the UN Security Council in January, it wasn't, in fact, until late April 1963 that the United States kept its part of the agreement between Khrushchev and Kennedy and removed its Jupiter missiles from Turkey and Italy. The first step was NATO's de-activation of the ballistic missiles on April 16; the 15 missiles in Turkey and the 30 in Italy were finally withdrawn from those countries on April 25. A U.S. Polaris submarine armed with nuclear weapons had begun patrolling the Mediterranean on April 1.

---

[147] Raúl Roa, letter to the United Nations, March 4, 1963. Translated from Spanish.
[148] Schlesinger, *Robert Kennedy*, 586.

By the end of April, everything that had been agreed upon in the negotiations concerning the crisis had been carried out. The missiles in Cuba and the IL-28 bombers were back where they had been in the beginning, and the naval blockade had been lifted. The only thing still unresolved was Washington's promise not to invade Cuba.

Fidel Castro had never been to the Soviet Union, and Nikita Khrushchev invited him to visit. The Cuban leader had gone through the traumatic experience of the crisis, and the way the conflict had been handled was still painful. The Cuban leader flew to Murmansk and then to Moscow in the spring of 1963, while the nuclear missiles were being removed from Italy and Turkey. During his three-week stay in the Soviet Union, he was feted in official circles, and the Soviet people expressed their solidarity with Cuba.

The crisis had not destroyed the links between the two countries. As proof of the soundness of their relations, during Fidel Castro's visit the two governments signed an agreement "on assistance for increasing the technical means of the Revolutionary Armed Forces and strengthening Cuba's defense capability." The Soviet Union pledged to supply Cuba free of charge with the weapons it needed, the only condition being that those weapons could not be turned over to third countries and that Cuba would not use the antiaircraft missiles against U-2s. A brigade of around 3,000 Soviet military personnel would be sent to Cuba; on their combat missions, they would take orders from Cuban officers, who would consult with the Soviet officers. Very beneficial agreements were also reached on economic matters and trade.

During the 1992 meeting held in Havana — a meeting attended by U.S., Soviet and Cuban experts — Fidel Castro made some key revelations about his talks with Khrushchev, on a hunting preserve in Zavidovo. Khrushchev let it slip that the missiles in Turkey and Italy were part of the agreement between the Kremlin and the White House. The Cubans hadn't known about this, because both the Soviet and U.S. leaders had kept it quiet.

Fidel Castro said that, for several hours, Khrushchev read messages that he had sent to President Kennedy through Robert Kennedy and Ambassador Thompson. Khrushchev, Fidel Castro and a translator who gave the Cuban leader a running translation of what Khrushchev was saying, were all sitting in a patio next to the house.

Fidel Castro recalled that scene as follows:

Khrushchev read and read. At one point, I thought he was saying something that wasn't of any interest I knew of... Nobody had underlined the key ideas in the texts, and there was one message he had received that said, "We have kept all of our promises... and have withdrawn, are withdrawing or will withdraw the missiles from Turkey and Italy"... I remember clearly that it spoke not only of Turkey but also of Italy... When I heard the message that Nikita was reading — that they were going to withdraw the missiles from Turkey and Italy — I thought, "Well! This hasn't been mentioned publicly; this must have been some kind of gift or concession." In this case, it was probably Kennedy helping Khrushchev, for there were times when Khrushchev wanted to help Kennedy and other times when he wanted to cause Kennedy inconvenience, or he did so without meaning to, and, at another time, Kennedy might be doing the same for Khrushchev... Nikita really mustn't have meant me to hear that. He knew what I thought, knew that I was utterly opposed to Cuba being used as a pawn for bargaining, which went against the idea that the missiles were for Cuba's defense. Cuba's defense didn't involve getting the missiles out of Turkey; that was perfectly clear and logical. Cuba's defense did involve saying, "Please take away the [Guantánamo Naval] base, please stop the economic blockade, no more pirate attacks, no more of this and that." But this thing contradicted the idea that the main purpose was the defense of Cuba. When that appeared and was read, I looked at him and said, "What? Please repeat." He read that part again, and I said, "The missiles from Turkey and Italy?" And he laughed, with that mischievous laugh of his. I am sure it had just slipped out; he hadn't meant to tell me that. He had simply put his foot in his mouth.[149]

At the end of the visit, they signed a communiqué which said that if Cuba was attacked in violation of the agreements between the Premier of the Soviet Union and the President of the United States, the Soviet Union would fulfill its international obligations to the people of Cuba and would offer the Republic of Cuba all the means at its disposal.

July 1963. The attacks on Cuba continued. On July 8, the U.S. Treasury Secretary froze all Cuban assets in the United States; prohibited all transfers of dollars to Cuba through third countries; gave third countries 60 days in which to cut off their trade with Cuba if they didn't want to incur economic and trade reprisals; blacklisted all the ships of capitalist countries which traded with Cuba, stating that they

---

[149] Tripartite Conference, January 11, 1992, fourth session, 54. Translated from Spanish.

would not be allowed in U.S. ports if they didn't heed this warning; and, through threats of sanctions, forced many countries to cancel the landing permits they had given for Cuban planes.

That wasn't all. The U.S. Treasury Department gave the impression it was acting in haste, without thinking, for it froze the funds of Cuba's Mission to the United Nations and the personal bank accounts of its members. This was a violation of the UN Charter and of the agreement between the United States and the United Nations which guaranteed the privileges and immunities of diplomats working at the United Nations and their independence in carrying out their functions. It was unprecedented. We denounced this high-handedness to the UN Secretary-General, saying that it was impossible to function normally in those conditions, lacking the freedom to move the funds assigned to the Mission, both to cover the expenses of the delegation and to meet the personal needs of its functionaries. We called for respect for our rights and said that the Mission would continue doing its duty, in spite of the difficulties placed in its path. We emphasized that Cuba's voluntary contribution of $50,000 to the Expanded Program of Technical Assistance had also been frozen. A few days later, Washington reversed that absurd measure.

In June, July, October and November 1963, Kennedy approved several programs of sabotage against important production centers, electric power plants and oil refineries in Cuba.

On the international scene, the process of détente advanced. A speech that Kennedy gave at American University in June indicated a change in the relations between the two powers and had great repercussions. It contained some ideas that had not been included in the vocabulary of the Cold War. The speech was mainly directed at the Soviet Union, offering it the prospect of beatific peace, "Not a Pax Americana enforced on the world by American weapons of war. Not the peace of the grave or the security of the slave.

"I am talking about genuine peace — the kind of peace that makes life on earth worth living, the kind that enables men and nations to grow and to hope and to build a better life for their children... Not merely peace in our time, but peace for all time."[150] The President paid homage to the sacrifices the Soviet people had made during World War II. "No nation had ever suffered more than the Soviet Union during the war."[151] Referring to the Missile Crisis that had just ended, he said that

---

150 Michael Beschloss, *The Crisis Years: Kennedy and Khrushchev, 1960-1963* (Edward Burlingame Books, 1991), 598.
151 Ibid., 599.

while defending its vital interests, each nuclear power should avoid confrontations that would place its adversary in a position of having to choose between a humiliating retreat or atomic war.

Ten days after that speech, the Soviet Union and the United States established a direct line of communication for messages between their top leaders, by means of a telegraph and telex circuit that ran through London, Copenhagen, Stockholm and Helsinki. On August 5, the diplomatic chiefs of the Soviet Union, the United States and the United Kingdom signed a partial nuclear test ban treaty in Moscow, ending underwater tests and tests in the atmosphere and outer space. The text said that it was a first step toward achieving general and total disarmament and completely prohibiting all atomic testing — none of which was achieved. It also included a pledge not to engage in nuclear testing for peaceful purposes and a pledge that the signatories would not participate in any way in such testing in other countries.

In October, Soviet and U.S. officials agreed that the United States would sell the Soviet Union a large amount of U.S. government-subsidized wheat.

10

The unknown

A s stated in the preceding chapter, McGeorge Bundy, who was closely linked to Kennedy, proposed in early 1963 that a rapprochement with the Cuban government should be considered. The first document mentioning that possibility was issued while the negotiators in New York were discussing the drafts of the documents to be submitted to the Security Council. By that time, Washington had already refused to support the protocol, rejected the individual declarations reflecting the positions of the three countries, turned down the idea of multiple inspections and was threatening to break off the dialogue with the Soviet Union if it insisted on having the Cubans participate in the final phase of the discussions. Dated January 4, 1963, this memorandum contained the initiative, which was mentioned only in passing, lumped with others that called for interfering in matters that were strictly Cuba's business. The suggestion was repeated on April 24.

I don't know what happened in the White House when the proposal was examined, because the documents which might throw some light on this matter have not been declassified. I don't know who supported the idea and who didn't, though it is clear that the military elements and the members of the intelligence community were committed to the subversive plans that would lead to a military invasion of Cuba. It is also clear that they nearly always prevailed over those who favored a more intelligent, responsible policy that was more in accord with détente. Nor do I know what stand the President took in those months, for no revelations have been made that show what he was thinking.

The only sure thing is that the attacks on Cuba continued throughout the year, the State Department and the Executive stepped up their diplomatic maneuvers to isolate Cuba politically, and the economic blockade was tightened with new measures. The alternatives to those who encouraged hostility were never publicized and didn't have enough weight to influence the established policy. It wasn't easy to take a new path. Enmity toward the Cuban revolution was deeply entrenched in the more reactionary sectors, which had enormous resources, political power in the Republican and Democratic parties and the last word in the mass media. They could mold public opinion to suit themselves, not only in the United States but also outside it, especially in Latin America, where most of the governments nearly always followed their northern neighbor's dictates.

The way in which the Missile Crisis was resolved stimulated those elements to continue with their aggression, pushing the subversive plans and closing off all possibilities of change. Those who favored modifying the policy followed since the Eisenhower era weren't strong enough to oppose this. Moreover, they had the same strategic aims of military domination, economic advantages and ideological penetration as the others, though by different means. This is why, when evaluating those internal contradictions in the light of historical events, it is difficult to say just what effect they might have had.

The step that Kennedy took toward exploring a rapprochement with Cuba was surprising in view of the prevailing situation, but it showed that, in some way, he wanted to crack the solid wall of intransigence toward revolutionary Cuba. He was taking a serious political risk, which is why the steps he took were known to only a small group of his closest collaborators; something that further indicates his uncertainty. The next year, he would be seeking reelection, and he didn't know who the Republican Party candidate would be — only that whoever it was would have a powerful weapon to use against him. Moreover, he would have to seek reelection not knowing how most of the voters would react, and the hawks in the military establishment would certainly oppose him. One thing that may have influenced his decision — all this is in the realm of speculation — was that the crisis was over and the path to détente with the Soviet Union was clear. The international situation was changing, even though the United States always viewed the question of Cuba differently from the way it viewed the rest of the world.

The General Assembly of the United Nations began its new session on the second Tuesday in September 1963. That was the setting Kennedy chose for initiating a rapprochement with the Cubans. People of all kinds wandered through the halls of the UN building next to the East River in New York. Diplomats, journalists, politicians and the curious filled the building. The Delegates Lounge was one of the most crowded places. At midday on September 23, Lisa Howard, a friend of Kennedy who worked for ABC television and had interviewed Fidel Castro in Cuba, came up to me and told me that Ambassador William Attwood of the U.S. delegation wanted to talk with me and that it was urgent, as he was going to Washington the next day. The journalist invited me to a party at her home that evening and said that it would be the best opportunity I would have for meeting with Attwood.

At that time, William Attwood was ambassador to Guinea and was in New York to advise the U.S. delegation. He was on very close terms with Ambassador Adlai Stevenson and had been one of his speech writers when Stevenson had run for president on the Democratic ticket. He also had close ties with President Kennedy — for whom he had also written speeches during his electoral campaign. He was close to those who wielded power. An outstanding journalist with long service, he had been an editor on *Look* magazine and then on *Newsday*, and he had interviewed Fidel Castro shortly after the 1959 triumph of the revolution.

The U.S. ambassador was introduced to me in the living room of Lisa Howard's home, in the midst of cocktails, sandwiches, diplomats and journalists. He lost no time in saying why he wanted to meet me. He said that Stevenson had authorized him to do so and that he would be flying to Washington in a few hours to request authorization from the President to go to Cuba to meet with Fidel Castro and ask about the feasibility of a rapprochement between Havana and Washington. He would go incognito and warned that he was speaking only as a private citizen, pending the instructions he would be given. He said that the situation was abnormal and that the ice would have to be broken sometime. He was very loquacious, and I could see that he wanted to establish an atmosphere of frankness to let me know that he was sincere. I told him that I, too, was speaking only as a private citizen but that I would tell my government and wait for its decision concerning his proposal. I added that, in view of the situation that existed between his country and mine and the fact that the United States policy of aggression had not abated, what he was telling me came as a surprise and that I would listen to him with great interest.

Attwood went on to say that he had two photos in his office in the U.S. embassy in Guinea: one of Fidel Castro waving from a plane and one of Fidel and his wife. One day, he invited the Soviet ambassador to dinner, and the Soviet diplomat had been surprised that the representative of the United States would have a picture of the Cuban leader in such an important place. He said that he had written two articles on Cuba which had been published in *Look* magazine in 1959 and that he had an idea that Havana hadn't been very pleased with the second one. He explained that, when he wrote it, he was influenced by a talk he'd had with Julio Lobo, a Cuban sugar magnate who lived in New York, who had invited him to the Savoy Plaza Hotel after Attwood had arrived back from Cuba. Lobo had told him he thought it would be good if Fidel Castro were assassinated — to which Attwood had replied that it would be a serious mistake, for it would result in a bloodbath, because Castro was very popular. From that conversation, Attwood had concluded that there was a large opposition movement in Cuba, which was what he reflected in his article.

He asked what the chances were that the Cuban government would allow him to go to Havana. I remember that I said I couldn't give him an official answer but that it was very possible. He then inquired if I felt the chances were 50-50. "That may be a good guess," I commented. He wanted to know what conditions would be required for negotiating. At that time, I couldn't tell him anything specific, but I said that my own view was that it would be difficult to negotiate in a situation of great pressure, such as there was in Cuba, with the economic blockade, the infiltration of saboteurs and the illegal flights. That atmosphere would have to be changed if the two parties were to discuss things on an equal footing, although, I repeated, everything would depend on what the United States wanted. He agreed that the situation was very complex, and he understood my point of view. He added that, someday, a process of rapprochement would have to begin, and he was convinced that it was useful to hear what I was telling him, even though I wasn't speaking in any official capacity.

He agreed that the political climate wasn't very propitious, since quite strong words had been exchanged, and he cited a recent speech of Fidel Castro. I replied that the words weren't strong at all but that the actions, hostility and harassment to which Cuba was subjected were. I recalled that after Kennedy's inaugural address, Fidel Castro had made some statements to the effect that there might be hope that Washington would give up its policy of aggression but that Kennedy had kept on attacking Cuba and had then launched the Bay of Pigs invasion. I recalled Kennedy's recent speech at American University which had a conciliatory tone, and then the violent attacks he had made later in a Berlin speech against the socialist countries, which was a contradiction. I mentioned that, two months earlier, the Treasury Department had frozen Cuba's funds in the United States and had even frozen the funds of the Cuban Mission to the United Nations. I reminded him that, after a partial nuclear test ban treaty had been signed in Moscow, the CIA had stepped up its infiltration of terrorist agents in Cuba and its spy flights and that it was trying to mobilize forces in Central America to use them in an attack. He agreed that all of it was true and that it was an absurd situation.

I asked him if the United States thought it could destroy the revolution. He replied that many members of the U.S. government were convinced of this. "The revolution is irreversible," I told him, and he replied that he didn't have any doubts about that and that many revolutions had taken place in the world. He said that he wasn't making any specific proposal, but that he was speaking with me because Stevenson had authorized him to do so and that he would see Kennedy the next day and didn't know if the President would authorize him to continue the dialogue or not. He said that Kennedy had inherited the problem of Cuba from Eisenhower and had no alternative but to follow the same policy, just as he had also inherited the problems of China and Vietnam. The situation on China was frozen, and even though he understood that it was absurd, it would take many years to change it. He added that Kennedy had often confessed in private conversations that he didn't know how he was going to change U.S. policy on Cuba, and that neither the United States nor Cuba could change it overnight because of the prestige involved. However, Kennedy said something had to be done about it and a start had to be made.

Attwood then made some interesting comments about U.S. domestic policy. He recognized that it wasn't easy for the Democrats to change course on Cuba, because the Republicans always had them on the defensive on the issue. He said that Barry Goldwater would probably be Kennedy's opponent in the next election, since Nelson Rockefeller had made many mistakes. Teasingly, he told me that if we thought Kennedy was our enemy, we should just imagine what Goldwater would do if he got to the White House.

Then he spoke of Robert Kennedy, saying that he held very strong positions but was a good politician and viewed things objectively. He said that the President's brother always wanted to win and that, if he thought the prolongation of the Cuba policy would have negative results, he would change his position.

Attwood thought that Kennedy would be reelected, but admitted that it would be a tough battle and that if he won by a narrow margin he wouldn't be able to carry out many of his projects. Attwood was worried about the racial problem, which at that time took the form of protest demonstrations, police repression and acts of violence by right-wingers. He said that in spite of the statements Kennedy had just made in defense of civil rights, he was being accused of not having acted effectively in the case of six young people in Alabama who were killed while participating in a memorial service. He was worried that the Republicans would adopt an intransigent position, with elements of the extreme right supporting Goldwater. In that case, the Democrats would be forced to take a position midway between the right and left, running the risk that the liberals might abstain from voting, which would benefit their opponents.

Returning to the subject of our meeting, Attwood referred to a talk that Averell Harriman, then Deputy-Secretary of State, had given not long before to the members of the U.S. Mission to the United Nations, in which Harriman had said that many agreements would be reached with the Soviet Union in the next 10 years. Even though he didn't mention Cuba by name, it was clear that he was referring to Cuba — at least, Attwood thought so — because Harriman had said that the agreements with Moscow would lead to understandings in other areas. Attwood then commented favorably on a speech that Gromyko had given recently, saying that peaceful coexistence was a positive thing.

At the end of our meeting, we spoke of his work in Guinea. He said that Sekou Touré was a good leader, a nationalist, who tried to be on good terms with everybody. He said he wasn't what many people in Washington thought him to be — a Soviet satellite or pro-West — and that people in the United States tended to see everything in terms of black and white, with no shadings.

Attwood insisted that he had contacted me on his own initiative, and he repeated this in two books that he published, but it is hard to believe that he would undertake such a delicate mission without having been asked to do so by people high up in the government. Be that as it may, Kennedy immediately came up in the conversation, and now that I know of the proposals made by Bundy, a very important figure in the White House, it is logical to think that the contact was the result of discussions in the inner circle around the Executive.

Attwood has said that he consulted with Harriman about meeting with me and that Harriman was interested and asked him to send a memo on the meeting. Later, Attwood discussed the possibility of the meeting with John Kenneth Galbraith, who was in New York after finishing his term as ambassador to India and was on his way back to Harvard to take up teaching again. Galbraith advised him to keep on talking with Harriman instead of Stevenson, because it was more likely the President would pay attention if he did so.[152] In any case, Attwood showed Stevenson the memo the next day, and Stevenson said, "unfortunately, the CIA is still in charge of Cuba."[153] Stevenson offered to speak with Kennedy to see if he would authorize the meeting with me. Attwood suggested that the best time for the encounter would be while the General Assembly was in session, since it was natural that he would speak with the Cuban ambassador, as he had visited Cuba in 1959.[154] On September 19, he gave a copy of the memorandum to Harriman, who was still in New York. Attwood reiterated that at that moment he needed authorization to meet with me, and Harriman offered to keep an eye on the project and advised him to speak with Robert Kennedy, because it was essential to get his approval. Attwood telephoned Robert Kennedy in Washington, and Kennedy said he would see him on September 24 (the day after the evening we met at Lisa Howard's house).

Meanwhile, Stevenson had already spoken with the President on September 20, when he arrived in New York to address the General Assembly, and Kennedy told him that Attwood should go ahead with the plan. Attwood said that for some reason Stevenson didn't want him to speak with Robert Kennedy, but he placed more trust in Harriman's instincts. Attwood flew to Washington on September 24, gave the memorandum to Robert Kennedy and told him about the meeting he'd had with me the night before. The President's brother told Attwood that his trip to Cuba, as proposed, was risky because news of it could leak out, and the least that might happen would be the Republicans accusing them of being appeasers and demanding a Congressional investigation. Robert Kennedy encouraged him to continue his contacts in the United Nations and said he would discuss the matter with Harriman and Bundy.

I had another meeting with Attwood on September 27, in the Delegates Lounge of the United Nations. He told me it was very difficult for him to go to Cuba because of his official post but that he was authorized to continue the talks. On October 2, Bundy called Attwood and told him that Gordon Chase, one of his deputies on the National Security Council, would be his contact in the White House

152 William Attwood, *The Twilight Struggle* (New York: Harper and Row, 1987), 258.
153 Ibid., 259.
154 Ibid.

and asked him to keep him informed about the progress of his talks with me.[155]

At that point, by chance, Jean Daniel, a French journalist who was then editor of the weekly *L'Observateur* and who was an old friend of Attwood, joined the project. The two had lunch together on October 3, and Daniel commented that he was in New York on his way to Washington and Havana. At that point, it occurred to Attwood to have Daniel talk with President Kennedy before going to Cuba and meeting with Fidel Castro. He called Ben Bradlee, *Newsweek* magazine's Washington correspondent, who was a friend of the President, visited the White House frequently and also knew Daniel, and asked him to try to set up a meeting for Daniel with Kennedy, which he did.

Four days after that meeting between Attwood and Daniel, I gave Cuba's main address in the General Assembly. It was the first General Assembly after the crisis, and 10 months had passed since the messages had been sent to the Security Council concluding the negotiations. I reviewed all the items on the agenda and said that the Cuban delegation would have liked to join in the prevailing optimism concerning the international situation, but that the realities which Cuba was confronting didn't allow us to do so. The atmosphere of intrigues and conspiracies which pervaded the Caribbean, as in the previous year, led us to a different viewpoint — the result of tangible facts and lamentable circumstances that adversely affected Cuba's independence and sovereignty, for Cuba was still the victim of covert intervention in its internal affairs and attacks by the United States.

I then read the long list of attacks that had been made against Cuba during the year and set forth Cuba's position on the Treaty of Moscow — on the partial banning of nuclear testing. I should note here that the Soviet government wanted Cuba to sign it, and the White House exhorted the Soviet diplomats to convince Havana to sign. In an interview Gromyko had with Kennedy five days after my address in the General Assembly, the President told him that his government would welcome the Cubans signing the Treaty; the Soviet Minister replied that Cuba had already stated its position in the United Nations.

Why didn't Cuba sign that pact? These were the reasons I gave on behalf of the revolutionary government:

• Cuba couldn't sign it because one of the signing powers had created a state of undeclared war against our country. During the Missile Crisis, the Cuban government had warned that there

---

[155] Ibid., 260.

would be no real peace for its people as long as the government of the United States persisted in grossly violating the Cuban people's most basic rights.

- The U.S. government maintained the economic blockade and was continuing to take measures all over the world to commercially and economically harass our country; it was continuing its subversive activities of dropping and landing weapons and explosives by air and sea and of infiltrating spies and saboteurs; it was still systematically violating Cuba's airspace and territorial waters; and it maintained the Guantánamo Naval Base, in defiance of our sovereignty.

- Cuba wouldn't sign the Treaty as long as the government of the United States continued those activities, even though its refusal to sign wouldn't, of course, affect the practical results of the Treaty. Cuba was not a nuclear power and lacked the resources to become one, but it was duty-bound to take a moral stand in the United Nations based on the inviolable principles of its international policy.

When I finished speaking, Ambassador Stevenson replied to the charges I had made against his government. He said he had hoped that the General Assembly had been freed of what he called immoderate Cold War rhetoric. He pointed out that one speaker after another had welcomed the new way of life on the international scene but that the speech by "the gentleman from Cuba" had been an exception. He spoke of Cuba's supposed subversive actions in Latin America and said that the United States denounced the use of its own territory for acts of violence against Cuba. (Yet, when Attwood had proposed the meeting with me, Stevenson himself had commented that, unfortunately, the CIA was still in charge of everything to do with Cuba.)

Curiously, it was William Attwood who wrote Stevenson's speech, but the incident didn't affect the contacts that had been established. [156]

On October 21, Gordon Chase, the contact in the White House, called Attwood in New York to ask if his efforts had borne any fruit. Attwood told him that he hadn't yet received any reaction from Havana. On October 28, I met again with the U.S. diplomat in the UN Delegates Lounge and told him that Havana was considering his proposal, but that it wasn't going to be possible for a high-ranking functionary of the Cuban government to go to the United States, even

---

[156] Ibid.

though somebody from Washington — possibly Attwood himself — would be welcome in our country.

As Attwood stated in his memoirs, Washington was giving more and more attention to talks with Cuba. Attwood kept Stevenson and Chase informed of all his contacts and was called to the White House on November 4 to talk with Bundy, who told him that the President was more interested in the matter than the State Department and asked him to write a memorandum describing, in chronological order, the contacts he had had, starting with his first conversation with Lisa Howard. Later, on November 12, Bundy called New York reminding him that the President was in favor of a preliminary discussion of the agenda for any meeting that might be arranged between an envoy of his and one of Fidel Castro's, either in Cuba or in the United Nations.

Without my knowledge, it seems that Lisa Howard — who had met Commander René Vallejo, aide to Prime Minister Castro, when she had been in Cuba — contacted him and asked him to take a call from Ambassador Attwood. In his memoirs, Attwood said that he spoke with Vallejo on November 18 and that Vallejo told him that Fidel Castro would send me instructions for discussing the agenda with Attwood in New York. Attwood informed Bundy of that conversation, and Bundy told him that as soon as the agenda was agreed upon Kennedy himself would speak with him to decide what he should tell Castro. He added that Kennedy was making a brief trip to Dallas but would be back in Washington soon.

A few days before that trip to Texas, the French journalist Daniel met with Kennedy at the White House. Daniel has written that he began the interview by asking the President if the ideas contained in his statements when he was a senator supporting the Algerian revolution had been faithfully applied in Saigon and in Havana.[157] The President said that he didn't have time to talk about Saigon, but that he wanted to talk about Cuba and continue the discussion when Daniel returned from Cuba. Kennedy commented that the European press accused the United States of being blind to the real situation in Cuba, but that he was perfectly aware of what was going on there. He criticized U.S. policy at the time of the Batista dictatorship and added that the problem was no longer a Cuban one but had become international — that is, a Soviet problem.

Daniel went to Cuba in November. In January 1992, in the meeting held in Havana, Fidel Castro revealed that he spoke with Daniel, who told him he had been very favorably impressed by

---

[157] *National Guardian*, December 19, 1963.

Kennedy and that he brought a message from him. The talk with Fidel
Castro took place at Varadero Beach.

It wasn't a message in the formal sense of the word. Rather,
Kennedy told him he wanted him to travel to Cuba. Kennedy
talked extensively about the crisis, about the enormous danger
that war would break out, the consequences of such a war and the
fact that he wanted Daniel to talk with me and analyze the matter,
and he asked him to ask me if I was aware of just how great the
danger had been. The essence of the message was that Daniel
should talk with me at length about all these things and then go
back to the United States and report to him about our talk.
Therefore, the journalist interpreted it as a gesture, as a wish to
establish contact, a wish to explore what we thought about all this
and also to establish communication. He told him to come here,
talk, analyze this problem and go back. That was the essence.

The journalist barely finished telling me everything he had to
say. It was very early — I think it was 11:00, Dallas time. It wasn't
even midday; we were going to have lunch, and, while we were
talking, making those assessments, the news came over the radio
that Kennedy had been seriously wounded in an assassination
attempt.

I interpreted Daniel's visit as a gesture to try to establish
communication, a bridge, a contact, because Kennedy had so
much authority inside his country after the crisis that he could do
things he might not have been able to do before. I think he had the
courage to do it — it took courage to defy established ideas on all
those things.

Later on, Fidel Castro commented:

Look at the paradox, the contradictions and coincidences: on the
same day and at the same hour that Jean Daniel was giving me
Kennedy's message, an agent of the United States was handing
over a fountain pen with a poison dart to be used in an
assassination attempt against me. Look how many paradoxes and
how many crazy things there are in the world![158]

---

[158] Fidel Castro, Tripartite Conference, fifth session, January 11, 1992, 13-15.
Translated from Spanish.

Fidel Castro was referring to Desmond FitzGerald, a high-ranking CIA officer who had replaced the ridiculous William Harvey as head of the CIA's center of subversion in Miami, and who gave the lethal pen to Rolando Cubela, a Cuban counterrevolutionary known as agent AM/LASH, whom the CIA was paying to commit the crime.

After Kennedy's death, Vice-President Lyndon Johnson moved into the White House. On November 29, Lisa Howard sent me a message from Attwood saying that the efforts hadn't been called off yet, that nobody in the White House had instructed him to break off the contacts. I spoke with Attwood on December 2, and he repeated what the journalist had told me. Gordon Chase told Attwood that he should be patient, as all policies were being reviewed. On returning to the United States from Cuba, Daniel saw Bundy and told him about his talk with Fidel Castro. On December 12, Attwood called me to say that Washington hadn't made a decision yet. That was the last time I spoke with him until some years later when we met in Havana, where he had come with his wife on an unofficial visit.

In his memoirs, Attwood said that when the new President went to New York to address the General Assembly he had lunch with the members of the U.S. delegation to the United Nations. He took the opportunity to tell Attwood that he had read with interest his memo on the efforts with Cuba, but didn't make any other comment. In January, Johnson named Attwood as ambassador to Kenya. While Attwood was in Washington preparing for his trip, Chase told him that the President's team of advisers didn't seem to be interested in doing anything with regard to Cuba in an election year.

He should have added that the government didn't want to do anything positive in line with international law, because Johnson immediately arranged for another country to join the economic blockade against Cuba. On December 24, Johnson went to Texas to spend the Christmas holidays on his ranch, and Ludwig Erhard, the new Chancellor of the Federal Republic of Germany, visited him there on December 28 and 29. They hunted deer. Johnson sold him a lot of military equipment in "payment" for having six divisions of the U.S. Army in Germany and wound up his negotiations with the German Chancellor by asking him to join the economic blockade against Cuba. The Chancellor agreed.[159]

The mystery surrounding Kennedy's assassination still remains. Many clues indicate a conspiracy to eliminate him before he could be

---

[159] Rowland Evans and Robert Novak, *Lyndon B. Johnson: The Exercise of Power* (New York: The New American Library, 1966), 389.

reelected, and well-founded speculation has it that the crime was moved forward because, as I have reported, he sought a rapprochement with the revolutionary government of Cuba, which might have resulted in a normalization of relations and the end of the U.S. policy of aggression. That may have tipped the scales in the decision to assassinate him. Historian Arthur Schlesinger, a collaborator of Kennedy's in the White House, thinks that the President's gesture of peace with Cuba was a factor in the death sentence that was decreed against him, and he refers to this in one of his books. Attwood, too, came to that conclusion. Three of the elements that are invariably mentioned as instruments in the assassination — the CIA, the Mafia and the Cuban counterrevolutionaries at the service of the CIA — were dead set against the normalization of relations with Cuba. Those three elements had already given abundant proof of their lack of scruples for undertaking an action of that kind and were irrevocably committed to the plans to destroy the revolution and to assassinate Cuban leaders.

As Schlesinger described it, "Though the Attwood plan was closely held, it seems inconceivable that the CIA knew nothing about it. American intelligence had Cuban UN diplomats under incessant surveillance. It followed their movements, tapped their telephone calls, read their letters, intercepted their cables. Suspecting, as it must have, that Attwood and Lechuga were doing something more than exchanging daiquiri recipes, the CIA, in pursuing the AM/LASH operation, must be convicted either of abysmal incompetence, which is by no means to be excluded, or else of a studied attempt to wreck Kennedy's search for normalization."[160] Robert Kennedy, the murdered President's brother, suspected the CIA of having had a hand in the assassination. When Jim Garrison, District Attorney of New Orleans, began making sensational accusations about a conspiracy, Schlesinger asked Robert Kennedy what he thought of those accusations, and Kennedy replied, "Garrison might be onto something."[161] NBC television sent journalist Walter Sheridan to New Orleans to investigate Garrison's accusations against the CIA, and Robert Kennedy talked with him and told him that he had asked CIA Director John McCone if the CIA had killed his brother. "At the time I asked McCone... if they had killed my brother, and I asked him in a way that he couldn't lie to

---

[160] Schlesinger, *Robert Kennedy*, 601.
[161] Ibid., 665.

me, and they hadn't."[162] But suspicions remained of the CIA's involvement.

In the memoirs he published in 1987, Attwood also said that the CIA must have found out about the efforts he was making and that later on information was fed to the frustrated veterans of the Bay of Pigs invasion, who hadn't lost hope of carrying out another attack protected by the CIA. Kennedy's feelers for normalizing relations with Cuba ended all their illusions.[163] Moreover, the Mafia had lost its gambling casinos, drug business and brothels when the revolution triumphed in Cuba, so the CIA had used it in the numerous attempts to kill Fidel Castro. The Mafia, too, had a stake in preventing an agreement between the two countries.

Almost 40 years have passed since the assassination in Dallas, and there is just as much speculation now as on the first day. Thus, the unforeseen consequences of the Missile Crisis claimed the life of the President of the United States.

---

[162] Ibid.
[163] Attwood, *The Twilight Struggle*, 264.

Also from Ocean Press

CIA TARGETS FIDEL
The secret assassination report
Only recently declassified and published for the first time, this secret report was prepared for the CIA on its own plots to assassinate Cuba's Fidel Castro.
ISBN 1-875284-90-7

SALVADOR ALLENDE READER
Chile's Voice of Democracy
Edited with an introduction by James D. Cockcroft
This book makes available for the first time Salvador Allende's voice and vision for a more democratic, peaceful and just world.
ISBN 1-876175-24-9

LATIN AMERICA: FROM COLONIZATION TO GLOBALIZATION
Noam Chomsky in conversation with Heinz Dieterich
An indispensable book for those interested in Latin America and the politics and history of the region.
ISBN 1-876175-13-3

CUBA — TALKING ABOUT REVOLUTION
Conversations with Juan Antonio Blanco
By Medea Benjamin
One of Cuba's outstanding intellectuals discusses Cuba today, featuring an essay, "Cuba: 'socialist museum' or social laboratory?"
ISBN 1-875284-97-7

CUBA AND THE UNITED STATES
A Chronological History
By Jane Franklin
This chronology relates in detail the developments involving the two neighboring countries from the 1959 revolution through 1995.
ISBN 1-875284-92-3

PSYWAR ON CUBA
The declassified history of U.S. anti-Castro propaganda
By Jon Elliston
Secret CIA and U.S. Government documents are published here for the first time, showing a 40-year campaign by Washington to use psychological warfare and propaganda to destabilize Cuba.
ISBN 1-876175-09-5

Also from Ocean Press

AFROCUBA
An anthology of Cuban writing on race, politics and culture
Edited by Pedro Pérez Sarduy and Jean Stubbs
What is it like to be Black in Cuba? Does racism exist in a revolutionary society that claims to have abolished it? *AfroCuba* looks at the Black experience in Cuba through the eyes of the island's writers, scholars and artists.
ISBN 1-875284-41-9

SLOVO
The unfinished autobiography of ANC leader Joe Slovo
A revealing and highly entertaining autobiography of one of the key figures of the African National Congress. As an immigrant, a Jew, a communist and guerrilla fighter — and white — few public figures in South Africa were as demonized by the apartheid government.
ISBN 1-875284-95-8

PRIEST AND PARTISAN
A South African journey of Father Michael Lapsley
By Michael Worsnip
The story of Father Michael Lapsley, an anti-apartheid priest who became the target of a South African letter bomb attack in 1990 in which he lost both hands and an eye.
ISBN 1-875284-96-6

I WAS NEVER ALONE
A Prison Diary from El Salvador
By Nidia Díaz
Nidia Díaz (born María Marta Valladares) gives a dramatic and inspiring personal account of her experience as a guerrilla commander during El Salvador's civil war. Seriously wounded, she was captured in combat by Cuban-exile CIA agent Félix Rodríguez. Nidia Díaz was the FMLN's Vice-Presidential candidate in 1999.
ISBN 1-876175-17-6

DEADLY DECEITS
My 25 Years in the CIA
By Ralph W. McGehee
A new, updated edition of this classic account of the CIA's deeds and deceptions by one of its formerly most prized recruits.
ISBN 1-876175-19-2

Also from Ocean Press

CHE GUEVARA READER
Writings on Guerrilla Strategy, Politics and Revolution
Edited by David Deutschmann
The most complete selection of Guevara's writings, letters and speeches available in English. As the most authoritative collection to date of the work of Guevara, this book is an unprecedented source of primary material on Cuba and Latin America in the 1950s and 1960s.
ISBN 1-875284-93-1

CHE — A MEMOIR BY FIDEL CASTRO
Preface by Jesús Montané
Edited by David Deutschmann
For the first time Fidel Castro writes with candor and affection of his relationship with Ernesto Che Guevara, documenting his extra-ordinary bond with Cuba from the revolution's early days to the final guerrilla expeditions to Africa and Bolivia.
ISBN 1-875284-15-X

CHE IN AFRICA
Che Guevara's Congo Diary
By William Gálvez
Che in Africa is the previously untold story of Che Guevara's "lost year" in Africa. Che Guevara disappeared from Cuba in 1965 to lead a guerrilla mission to Africa in support of liberation movements. The story behind the Congo mission is now revealed, reprinting Guevara's previously unpublished Congo Diary.
ISBN 1-876175-08-7

CHE GUEVARA AND THE FBI
U.S. political police dossier on the Latin American revolutionary
Edited by Michael Ratner and Michael Steven Smith
A Freedom of Information case succeeded in obtaining Che Guevara's FBI and CIA files, which are reproduced in this book. These sensational materials add to suspicions that U.S. spy agencies were plotting to assassinate Guevara in the 1960s.
ISBN 1-875284-76-1

Also from Ocean Press

JOSE MARTI READER
Writings on the Americas
An outstanding new anthology of the writings, letters and poetry of one of the most brilliant Latin American leaders of the 19th century.
ISBN 1-875284-12-5

FIDEL CASTRO READER
The voice of one of the 20th century's most controversial political figures — as well as one of the world's greatest orators — is captured in this new selection of Castro's key speeches over 40 years.
ISBN 1-876175-11-7

CUBAN REVOLUTION READER
A Documentary History
Edited by Julio García Luis
An outstanding anthology presenting a comprehensive overview of Cuban history and documenting the past four decades, highlighting 40 key moments in the Cuban Revolution up to the present day.
ISBN 1-876175-10-9
Also available in Spanish (ISBN 1-876175-28-1)

WASHINGTON ON TRIAL
Cuba's $181 billion claim against the U.S. government for war crimes
Introduced by Michael Ratner and David Deutschmann
ISBN 1-876175-23-0

CAPITALISM IN CRISIS
Globalization and World Politics Today
By Fidel Castro
Cuba's leader adds his voice to the growing international chorus against neoliberalism and globalization.
ISBN 1-876175-18-4

Ocean Press, GPO Box 3279, Melbourne 3001, Australia
● Fax: 61-3-9329 5040 ● E-mail: edit@oceanpress.com.au

www.oceanbooks.com.au